Building bridges:
multilingual resources for children

Bilingual education and bilingualism

Series Editor
Professor Colin Baker, University of Wales, Bangor

Other books in the series

Other books of interest

Please contact us for the latest book information:
Multilingual Matters Ltd
Frankfurt Lodge, Clevedon Hall, Victoria Road, Clevedon, Avon, BS21 7SJ

Bilingual education and bilingualism 4
Series Editor: Colin Baker

Building bridges:
multilingual resources for children

Multilingual Resources for Children Project

Multilingual Matters Ltd
Clevedon – Philadelphia – Adelaide

Published by
• Multilingual Matters Ltd

    UK Frankfurt Lodge, Clevedon Hall, Victoria Road, Clevedon, Avon, England BS21 7SJ

    USA 1900 Frost Road, Suite 101, Bristol, PA 19007, USA

    Australia PO Box 6025, 83 Gilles Street, Adelaide, SA 5000, Australia

• Reading & Language Information Centre, The University of Reading, Bulmershe Court, Earley, Reading, RG6 1HY

• Department of Typography & Graphic Communication, The University of Reading, 2 Earley Gate, Whiteknights, PO Box 239, Reading, RG6 2AU

© 1995 Multilingual Resources for Children Project

Designed and produced by Text Matters

Printed in Great Britain by Biddles Limited

Library of Congress cataloging in publication data

Building bridges: multilingual resources for children / Multilingual Resources for Children Project

          p.   cm.   (Bilingual education and bilingualism: 4)

Includes bibliographical references.

ISBN 1 – 85359 – 290 – 0 (pbk)

1. Education, bilingual – Great Britain. 2. Language and education – Great Britain. 3. Multicultural education – Great Britain. 4. Teaching – Aids and devices. 5. Bilingual books – Great Britain. 6. Typography I. Multilingual Resources for Children Project. II. Series

LC3736. G6B85   1995

371. 97 0941 – DC20   94 – 46504 – CIP

British Library cataloguing in publication data

A CIP catalogue record for this book is available from the British Library

ISBN 1-85359-290-0 (pbk)

Contents

Preface

The starting point for this book is The Multilingual Resources Project for Children carried out at The University of Reading, UK in the Departments of Arts and Humanities in Education and Typography & Graphic Communication.

We use the term 'multilingual' to refer to the society in which we live and specifically to mean the main languages other than English that are used in the UK: Bengali, Chinese, Gujarati, Panjabi and Urdu. The 'resources' we consider in the Project, mainly books and materials for reading, are generally not multilingual, but bilingual (as in a dual language book) or single language, non-English editions. We also consider resources to encourage speaking and listening in other languages, and finally, we stress the importance of writing as a resource in multilingual classrooms. The 'children' in the Project title were observed in two main settings: language classes organised by minority communities for children aged from 5–16, and state infant, junior and primary schools for children between the ages of 5 and 11.

The Project therefore has a specific context. The discussion, however, has relevance well beyond the UK for multilingual publications, for instance, in Australia, New Zealand, North America and many European countries.

The Project also brings together ideas from three disciplines: education, linguistics and typography. This interdisciplinary mix has been the fermentation ground for new perspectives on using and producing resources in and for multilingual schools. Further diversity occurs in the constituency of the research team: Khalida Alvi, Ruth Blacksell, Urmi Chana, Shobana Devani, Viv Edwards, Trilokesh Mukherjee, Ira Saxena, Amy Thompson and Sue Walker. This team brings together not only speakers of all the Project languages, but also teachers, typographers and linguists.

Hodgson & Saronak (1987, p. 20) write of the value of working together:

> ... it is necessary to cross the boundaries which traditionally have separated the various disciplines devoted to language phenomena. Fields as diverse as sociolinguistics, the comparative study of two or more languages, as well as typography and the analysis of literary texts – all have a contribution to make to the study of 'languages in contact and/or conflict'.

The Multilingual Resources for Children Project can also claim to represent 'languages in contact' – interaction between mono- and bilingual children through speaking, listening, reading and writing. We also experienced 'languages in conflict' when, in a bilingual text, one language has lower status by inappropriate translation or different typographic treatment to the other. The perspectives which we offer on both languages in contact and languages in conflict have, without a doubt, gained in breadth and depth through this interdisciplinary, multi-professional and multilingual collaboration.

Acknowledgements

The Multilingual Resources for Children Project could not have happened without the expertise, commitment and support of the members of the research team: Khalida Alvi, Ruth Blacksell, Urmi Chana, Shobana Devani, Trilokesh Mukherjee, Ira Saxena, and Amy Thompson. We particularly acknowledge the contribution of Ruth Blacksell and Urmi Chana who organized and carried out the fieldwork in the schools, and presented the findings in an exemplary way.

Our thanks to the teachers and children in the fieldwork schools: Thomas Buxton Junior, Barham Primary, Cranford Infant, and Havelock Primary; and classes at the Ahmadiyya Muslim Women's Association, the Darpan Bengali School, the Ramgarhia Sabha Sunday School and the Hounslow Chinese School. Our fieldworkers appreciated the welcome they received and the help they were given. We would also like to thank staff and children at Redlands Primary, Reading, and Penny Kenway for allowing us to draw on work she conducted at Wellington Primary, west London.

Many others contributed to the Project. We would like to thank the members of our steering group who provided helpful advice at the start of the Project: Clem Adelman, Alan Rogers, Pat Norrish; and Angela Redfern and Michael Twyman for their ongoing support. Chris Abbott, Sandip Hazareesingh, Pauline Silcock and Shahida Usman of South West Herts Language and Curriculum Support Centre, Karel van der Waarde and Joti Tammli provided stimulating and thought-provoking contributions to our working group meetings. Our thanks to Richard Raby for his help in answering queries about multilingual word-processing and in providing illustrations. Judith Powell and Brenda Tucker provided invaluable administrative support. We are grateful to The University of Reading Research Endowment Fund for funding the two-year Project.

We are also grateful to Mark Barratt and Angela Redfern for their diligent reading of the final draft, and to Sally Adkins for care and attention to detail in designing the book. Responsibility for the writing of the final text, however, has been ours as Project directors. We are conscious we have written from our own perspectives – those of a linguist and a typographer – and although we have drawn heavily on the material provided/contributed by the research group, we are aware that it is all too easy with a subject of such complexity for occasional errors of detail and judgement to slip in. If such anomalies have arisen, the fault is ours.

Viv Edwards
Sue Walker

Acknowledgements to publishers

We are grateful to the following publishers for permission to reproduce pages from their books. If not given here, full publication details, author, illustrator and translator are given in the captions to the pictures.

Walker Books Limited for an excerpt from *Can't you sleep, Little Bear?* Text © 1988 Martin Waddell. Illustrations © 1988 Barbara Firth. Published in the UK by Walker Books Limited and in the US by Candlewick Press, Cambridge MA. Child's Play (International) Ltd for a page from *Veloce come un grillo* written by Audrey Wood, illustrated by Don Wood (1982). Roy Yates Books for pages from *Star children's picture dictionary, Spot goes to the farm* by Eric Hill (Chinese/English edition, 1989). Ingham-Yates Associates for a page from *Dear Zoo* by Rod Campbell (Panjabi/English edition, 1987). Magi Publications for pages from the following dual texts: *The eagle that would not fly* by James Aggrey (1988), *Princess Smartypants* by Babette Cole (1992), *Can't you sleep, Little Bear?* by Martin Waddell and Barbara Firth (1993), *Getting dressed* by Kati Teague (1989), and *Anita and the magician* by Swaran Chandan (1987). Jennie Ingham for pages from *The tiger and the woodpecker* by Aruna Ajitsaria (1984), *The hare and the tortoise* by Gabriel Douloubakas (1985), and *The enchanted palace* by Ashim Battacharya and Champaka Basu (1985). Jennie Ingham and Prodeepta Das for a page from *Me playing* (1987). Jennie Ingham and Cambridge University Press for a page from *A wet dinner time* (1989). Partnership Publishing for pages fom *The moving mango tree* by Zohra Jabeen (1992) and *Send for Sohail!* by Grange Road First School (1993). Harmony Publishing Ltd for pages from *Sameep and the parrots* by Elaine Abrahams (1986). Penguin Books Ltd for a page from *The snowman* by Raymond Briggs (Puffin Books, 1980); first published in 1978 by Hamish Hamilton Children's Books Ltd. Jennie Ingham and Macdonald Young Books Ltd for a page from *Frogs* (1987). Scholastic Publications Ltd for a page from the English/Panjabi, English/Gujarati and English/Urdu editions of *Shan helps Rani* by Mary Dickenson (1990) (André Deutsch Children's Books is an imprint of Scholastic Publications Ltd). Mantra Publishing Ltd for pages from the following dual texts: *Woman with the pushchair* by Steve Kaufman (1993), *The magic ink* by Anna Robinson (1986), *The first rains* by Peter Bonnici (1984), *Lights for Gita* by Rachel Gilmore (1994), *Do you believe in magic* by Saviour Pirotta (1991). Methuen Educational Ltd for a double page spread from the English/Panjabi edition of *School dinners* by Peter Heaslip. *Le tunnel* by Brian Wildsmith (1993) is reproduced by permission of Oxford University Press.

We have made every effort to contact all the publishers of the material we have reproduced. In some cases we have failed because addresses have changed and people have moved on. This has been the case especially in relation to materials published by community groups. We would like to apologize for not making contact, but hope that inclusion in our publication indicates the importance and value we attach to such materials.

I Life with many languages

Life with many languages

There is nothing strange or exotic about speaking more than one language. From a global perspective, multilingualism is the norm; even countries with one official language have a multilingual heritage. Welsh, Irish, Gaelic, Cornish, Manx, French, Norn, Shelta and Polari are all part of the fabric of the British Isles. France is home to Breton, Catalan, Basque, Italian, German and Dutch as well as French. Yet, all too often, multilingualism has been overlooked or marginalized in national policy and planning.

The scale of population movement in the second half of the twentieth century has made it increasingly difficult to justify monolingual myopia. A language census carried out in London schools in the late 1980s showed that children spoke a total of 172 different languages. The 1989 US Census of Population reported eight languages other than English with over half a million speakers (McArthur, 1993). Meanwhile in Australia, Horvath & Vaughan (1991) document some fifty-eight different languages. And, as countries like Canada and Australia have abandoned their 'whites only' immigration policies, linguistic minorities have also become increasingly visible minorities. In classrooms populated by children who speak many languages in addition to English, the resources which teachers offer need to reflect the multilingual reality of their daily lives.

This book has been written with several audiences in mind: teachers in community and mainstream schools who recognize the potential of multilingual resources, as well as the writers, translators, designers and publishers responsible for producing them. The examples which we use come mainly from our experiences in British schools, but the issues which we raise will be recognized by teachers in multilingual classrooms all over the world.

Responses to diversity

Various factors have been responsible for population movements since the Second World War. On the one hand, host countries are viewed as offering better economic prospects or a refuge from political oppression. But, on the other hand, migrants are responding to the need for labour in their new country and, in many cases, have taken on low-paid work with anti-social hours which has little appeal for established populations.

Reactions to immigrants tend to vary over time. The host community's initial impulse is to assimilate newcomers. This policy is summed up in the American metaphor of the melting pot: individual allegiances must be abandoned in the pursuit of a supra-national identity. In this view, English (or French, or Dutch or whatever the language of the dominant group) must be taught to the exclusion of all other languages and newcomers must accommodate to mainstream customs and expectations. But the continued presence of Polish-Americans, Italian-Americans, Irish-Americans and so on has challenged the myth of cultural homogeneity. While migrants are happy to learn new ways, they are naturally attached to their own languages and cultures. Their goal is to add the new language to their repertoire, not to shed the old one. And, in situations where different groups of people have unequal access to power and wealth, linguistic and cultural markers become the symbol of resistance. They are not abandoned at a whim.

Over time, this kind of pressure from minority groups has led to a rather different response to diversity, known variously as integration, cultural pluralism or multiculturalism. The notion is that, if settlers are to compete on equal terms, linguistic and cultural differences must be recognized and celebrated. The transition from assimilation to multiculturalism created a new climate of opinion in many countries: legal cases such as Lau v. Nichols (see, for instance, Scarcella, 1990) paved the way for bilingual education programmes in America; many British schools made community languages like Urdu and Panjabi part of the curriculum; and, when petitioned by ten or more parents, Boards of Education in Ontario are now obliged to provide heritage language teaching in the language requested. The new philosophy is summed up in the Canadian metaphor of the salad bowl: the various ingredients retain their integrity at the same time as creating a more interesting whole. Sadly, this image has proved as unsatisfactory as the melting pot. The growing evidence of discrimination and educational underachievement (see Cummins & Danesi, 1990) might lead cynical observers to conclude that Canadians are trying to make a uniformly green salad.

Again, pressure from minorities is forcing us to reassess the situation. Many educators now recognize that equality requires much more than the celebration of diversity: we also need to look critically at aspects of school and society which favour some groups over others. Unfortunately, arguments for anti-racist education are taking place against a right wing backlash: the rise of neo-nazism in Europe; the introduction in England and Wales of a curriculum which stresses a national culture and language; and moves within the USA to establish English as the official language.

Minority perspectives

The discussion so far has centred on the dominant group's reactions. What, then, of minority perspectives? Again, it is possible to trace similar patterns of response from one country to another. In the early days, the stresses of finding work and accommodation and generally adjusting to life in a new country preoccupy the settlers. They are understandably concerned that they – and their children –

should learn to speak English (or French, or German, or Dutch ...) as rapidly as possible. After some time (and often as children born in the new country reach adolescence), parents realize that a gap has opened up. Children have shifted from the language of the home to English and communication between them and their parents and grandparents becomes increasingly difficult.

It is usually at this point that individuals look for help beyond the family to the minority community as a whole. Religious groups often take a prominent role in the setting up of language classes: the Orthodox church for Greek, gurdwaras for Panjabi, mosques for Urdu and so forth. In some cases, embassies and High Commissions also support their citizens overseas. Where minority communities are large and have political clout, bilingual programmes and after-school classes often receive official assistance. Sometimes the motives for official intervention are dubious. The European Union, for instance, has justified the provision of mother tongue teaching on the grounds that, should economic conditions make it necessary to repatriate 'guest workers', children will be able to make the necessary adjustments more easily.

Whatever the motivation, there is enormous interest in and support for community or heritage language teaching. To take just two examples, classes in eighteen different languages were being offered to over 8,500 pupils in just three English local education authorities (LMP, 1985); just a few years later, the Canadian Ethnocultural Council (1988) reported that seventy-two school boards in Ontario were offering 4,364 classes in fifty-eight different languages to 91,110 students.

The level of resourcing in these classes varies enormously from country to country and from one community to the next. Canadian heritage language classes have access to free accommodation, and teachers'

salaries are paid from local taxes. In Britain, only a small proportion of classes receive official support: in some cases, they are offered accommodation free of charge or at subsidized rates; in some cases teachers' salaries are paid. Only rarely are both salaries and accommodation provided and, in most cases, teachers receive only their travel expenses (LMP, 1985).

Teachers tend to come from a wide range of backgrounds: some taught in the country of origin; some work as teachers in the new country. For many others, the main qualification is that they speak the language. There is a serious shortage of in-service training for community language teachers; access to books and other materials is also limited (Edwards & Redfern, 1992).

Relationships between teachers in community classes and mainstream schools are also a matter of concern. Community language teachers using mainstream school premises talk of the frustration which they feel when they are surrounded by resources which would be useful in their own teaching, but which are out of bounds. Mainstream teachers complain bitterly that their classrooms have been disturbed and that items have gone missing. Many such complaints are without foundation. A superintendent in Metropolitan Toronto reported that the damage caused by community classes for an entire school year amounted to only fifty dollars (Edwards & Redfern, 1992). Sadly, many discussions about language classes centre on territorial concerns rather than on children.

Building bridges in the classroom

Linguistic diversity, of course, is not the exclusive domain of community language teaching; it is also a matter of great interest in mainstream schooling. The literature is full of examples of how minority languages can be used to help children consolidate language and literacy learning in the first language and accelerate development in English. Book making, small group discussions, drama – these are just some of the activities which allow children to use their home languages, both in mainstream classes and in 'withdrawal' classes for English as a second language.

In the UK, the prevailing feeling is that the mainstream classroom offers the richest language learning environment. Whereas children learning English as a second language were previously placed in special centres and classes, they are now taught in the mainstream where, ideally, language support teachers work in partnership with class and subject teachers. In schools where many of the children share the same minority language background, bilingual support teachers and instructors are encouraged to use children's home language as a bridge to the acquisition of English. The use of the home language can also give access to the curriculum.

Teachers are gradually attuning to the possibilities which multilingual classrooms offer. The use of other languages gives bilingual children status by allowing them to demonstrate their skills. It also has cognitive and academic advantages. We used to think that the brain had a finite capacity, and that children who learned two or more languages could not achieve the same level of proficiency as monolingual children. More recently, we have come to understand that the cognitive skills necessary for activities such as reading and writing are transferred from one language to another. They don't have to be learned afresh. We also have a clearer view of the importance of a sound foundation in the first language for development in other languages (Cummins, 1994; Ramirez, 1992).

At the same time, the presence of other languages in the classroom is of value to monolingual children. It helps them develop their 'knowledge about language' (DES, 1988) through an understanding that speakers of different languages express themselves with a different range of sounds, different words and different constructions and, on many occasions, using different writing systems. It also broadens their view of what it means to live in a multicultural society and in an increasingly interdependent world.

The changing composition of classrooms is reflected not only in learning experiences but also in the resources offered to children. Many books on multilingual classrooms make reference to learning materials. However, the most common emphasis is on issues such as cultural content: are children from a variety of ethnic backgrounds represented? Does the author avoid stereotypes? Do minority characters take a central role or do they merge into the background? It is also the case that discussion usually focusses on books in English.

Building bridges attempts to extend the debate on resources in new directions. An important first step is to change the focus from English to a range of other languages, reflecting the multilingual composition of many city schools. We examine the range and quality of resources in other languages in school and ways to use them. Of course, this discussion takes place within a social and political context. The exclusive focus on sarees, samosas and steel bands no longer has a place. Tokenistic gestures to include elements from other cultures have little or no impact on educational outcomes for minority children. For this reason, our exploration of multilingual resources assumes that it is not enough to place books in other languages on library shelves; we also need to look to the attitudes, ethos and organization which encourage their effective use.

Design issues

Teachers very often overlook the importance of design and typography on the effectiveness and usability of multilingual resources. *Building bridges* attempts to redress this imbalance by raising key issues that are important in selecting and producing materials in different languages.

There has been considerable research on the place of illustration in the teaching of reading (see Goldsmith, 1984) and a growing recognition that typography in children's books – choice of typeface, use of space and book conventions – needs careful consideration (Walker, 1992). Add another language to a book, and turn a monolingual text into a dual text, and there are other issues. Dual texts provide an opportunity to explore the interface between language and typography in two senses: getting the representations of two languages to work on the page, and for a specific group of users: young readers. In a dual text the typography of the two languages has to work well for children; so does the relationship of the two languages, and the relationship of the texts to the pictures. Without care in the organization of such elements, one language can appear more important than the other.

Even in languages that use the Latin alphabet, there can be visual anomalies. A typeface which works well in English, for instance, can have a different visual effect in other Latin-script languages, and may even reduce the legibility of the text (Szanto, 1972). When Latin and non-Latin fonts are combined in the same document, there are other concerns. Lubell (1993), for instance, raises some of the issues involved in trying to typeset Hebrew and non-Hebrew texts: problems of alignment, directionality and use of graphic conventions. These are some of the issues that we will return to later in relation to the languages of the Project schools – Bengali, Chinese, Gujarati, Panjabi and Urdu.

The Multilingual Resources for Children Project

Support for a project on 'Multilingual resources for children' came from The University of Reading Research Endowment Fund. The Project grew out of the collaboration of a typographer and a specialist in language and education. The interdisciplinary nature of the research proved challenging from the outset. Our first intentions were to appoint as assistant an experienced bilingual teacher with a knowledge of typography. Not surprisingly, such an individual proved elusive and a compromise was called for. Instead, we appointed a typographer to the position of half-time research officer and used the remaining funding to convene a working group of representatives from the five main linguistic minorities in the UK (Bengali, Chinese, Gujarati, Panjabi and Urdu). Four members of this group were teachers, and the fifth, a typographer. We also enlisted the support of a Hindi-speaking children's writer temporarily resident in England. We had, therefore, assembled a group of people whose knowledge and experience would most certainly have outshone the bilingual teacher-typographer we had initially hoped for.

In the first part of the two-year Project, each working group meeting explored particular themes: school ethos; the visual environment; translation; relative placement of illustrations and text in dual language books; low resolution word-processing for non-Latin scripts. As the fieldwork progressed, the working group offered feedback on preliminary findings and offered suggestions as to other directions which might be explored.

Fieldwork took place in four mainstream and five community schools in and around London. Two of the mainstream schools were primary (catering for children from five to eleven years of age); one was an infant school (for children between the ages of five and seven); and one a junior school (for children of seven to eleven). We decided to concentrate on schools for younger children because, in our experience, attempts to meet the needs of bilingual pupils are better developed here than in the secondary sector.

The language backgrounds of children varied from school to school: the overwhelming majority of children at Thomas Buxton Junior School came from Bangladesh; most children at Barham Primary School were Gujarati speakers from India and East Africa; Cranford Infant School and Havelock Primary School had substantial numbers of Sikh and Moslem children from the Panjab. The proportion of linguistic minority children varied from ninety-eight per cent at Thomas Buxton to sixty per cent at Cranford.

We have also drawn on the experience of several other mainstream schools in Britain

and Canada. Although these schools were not specifically included in the project, they are well-known to members of the research team. Two of us are parents at Redlands Primary School, a multilingual primary school in southern England which was the focus for an earlier study by Edwards & Redfern (1988). Various Canadian schools in Etobicoke, part of Metropolitan Toronto, provided a useful point of comparison with the UK situation, as previously reported in Edwards & Redfern (1992). We have also been able to use case studies of work conducted at Wellington Primary School in west London by Penny Kenway (1994).

The community language schools included in the present study were chosen to represent a range of languages similar to those found in the mainstream Project schools. We observed and interviewed teachers and children in Urdu classes at the Ahmadiyya Muslim Women's Association; in Gujarati classes organized by the Brent Indian Association; in Bengali classes at the Darpan Bengali School; and Panjabi classes at the Ramgarhia Sabha Sunday School. Because the Chinese population is more dispersed, it was not possible to identify a mainstream school with substantial numbers of Chinese children. We did, however, visit the Hounslow Chinese School.

Creating the right ethos

While good resources are necessary conditions for success, they are not enough in themselves. What happens when multilingual resources are introduced into the classroom? In chapter two, we take the position that books in other languages offer cognitive benefits and raise the status of bilingual pupils, at the same time as broadening the horizons of their monolingual peers. But such developments can only take place in schools where linguistic diversity is treated as an asset, not a problem; and where teachers recognize that appropriate resources are not an answer in themselves, but just one part of the solution.

What conditions, then, need to be in place to ensure that books in other languages aren't simply an exotic extra, decorating library shelves? We start by looking at the attitudes and ethos which need to be in place if multilingual materials are to make a positive impact on children's learning. We look, too, at practical aspects of school organization essential to the success of multilingual resources, from the visual environment to policies on equal opportunities. And we explore the relationship between home and school and ways in which parents and older siblings can help produce and promote resources in other languages.

Speaking and listening

Our original Project focus was on the written word, but as we talked to teachers and children and observed a range of classroom practice, it seemed very natural to extend the brief to speaking and listening. We start in chapter three by exploring negative views towards minority languages which have been common among teachers and why these views have been challenged in recent times. We offer a broad interpretation of 'resources', recognizing that bilingual children, teachers and other

adults working in the classroom are by far the most important resource. And we address a number of practical questions: how can the use of children's home languages enhance their learning? In what ways do teachers set about bilingual storytelling and drama? How can groups and individual children be encouraged to use – and produce – audio and videocassettes? Drawing on examples of work in school, we make recommendations for effective practice.

Reading

The reading resources found in many multilingual schools and communities form the focus for chapter four. In the local environment, these include shop signs, posters and labels in shop windows. In the school, there may also be a wide range of books, produced by children, parents and teachers as well as by commercial publishers.

Commercial publishers are responsible for two main kinds of books: single language and dual language. Single language books come from a variety of sources: mainstream and community publishers, projects which promote lesser-used languages, as well as bookshops which specialize in imported materials.

Some imported books raise difficult questions. Teachers often complain that materials produced abroad, particularly in the Indian sub-continent, are not of comparable quality to books produced in North America, Britain, Australia, New Zealand or Hong Kong. Are perceptions of 'quality' specific to a given culture, or are criteria for excellence more universal? And to what extent do children and parents share the views of teachers on this matter?

While single language books are usually associated with community or heritage language schools, dual language books written in English and another language are by far the most common multilingual resource in mainstream classrooms. They also pose the greatest number of challenges for teachers and designers. Do typographic features such as size or spacing mean that one script takes precedence over the other? Is one script of a higher quality than the other? What status messages do differences of this kind send out? And how do children actually use dual language texts? Do they read one language or both? How do teachers use and promote these books? We examine how these resources are used in schools. We look, too, at the range of problems which they pose – cost, quality and availability to name just a few – and at the different requirements of community and mainstream teachers.

One key issue – translation – affects both single language and dual language books. In different language versions of the same book, or in dual language books, is the translation of

the English text appropriate? For instance, are they of the same level of difficulty or formality? And which language – or dialect – is the most appropriate for any given community?

In exploring these and other questions, we have consulted both teachers and children. The articulate and sensitive responses from children have proved particularly illuminating, sometimes contradicting views commonly put forward by teachers.

Writing

Other languages are an important part not only of children's reading diet but also of their writing, a question which we explore in chapter five. Most of the materials which we consider under the heading of 'reading' are produced by commercial publishers. However, it would be short-sighted to overlook the fact that a great deal of children's reading material in other languages is generated in the school by teachers, parents and the children themselves.

The importance of bilingual adults – whether responding to children's writing or producing materials of their own – cannot be overestimated, especially in classes where the teacher is monolingual. Bilingual children need the opportunity to consolidate writing skills in both their languages; monolingual children benefit from exposure to a variety of languages and scripts.

Most children's work will be handwritten. Different kinds of handwriting, including the calligraphic traditions of Perso-Arabic and Chinese scripts, provide a valuable broadening of experience. But much work intended for a wider audience will draw on other modes. Until quite recently, the text of languages with Latin scripts was usually typed, while non-Latin scripts, like the Devanagari used for Hindi, or the Gurmukhi script for Panjabi, were handwritten. However, the

wider availability of word processors and multilingual word-processing packages is opening
up exciting new possibilities.

A multilingual heritage

Finally, in chapter six, we draw together
the various threads which weave their way
through the book: the value of diversity for
all children in all schools; the importance of
creating an ethos which supports the use of
multilingual resources; the need to recognize
status issues associated with language and the
design and production of resources; the fact
that children are far more perceptive users of
material than they are generally given credit
for; and the potential of resources for building
bridges between monolinguals and bilinguals,
between home and school.

2   Creating the right ethos

Many teachers are anxious to promote an understanding of cultural diversity in the children they teach. They need no persuasion about the vital role that carefully selected materials play in this process. However, experience has shown that, while teacher commitment and good resources are necessary conditions for success, they are not enough in themselves. If we want to create an effective learning environment, we also need to look to the attitudes, ethos and organization which encourage their use.

An understanding of cultural diversity

Diversity is an emotive issue and discussions often centre on why it is so difficult to address in schools. The following are a selection of comments that teachers sometimes make.

'The children in my class say they only speak English'

Children are very aware that minority languages are usually low status. Tales abound of children being told to 'stop jabbering in Gujarati' or even being asked to pay a fine when they are heard speaking the home language in school. Teachers consulted during the course of the Project were clear that some progress has been made. Multilingual resources are now in place in many schools and there is evidence of a growing appreciation of the advantages of bilingualism.

However, many mainstream teachers still feel that community language teaching may confuse children; and some teachers report children's embarrassment and lack of confidence in using their home language in public. One bilingual teacher consulted during the Project explained the situation thus:

> When we have assemblies ... to celebrate the children's own cultures and religions, they're embarrassed to come up on stage to speak, to act, to show what they are, what they belong to ... the older they get, the worse it becomes because they haven't got the confidence, the knowledge ... that they've got an identity and they can be proud of it.

Another symptom of the low status of minority languages is children's tendency to use inaccurate terminology (see LMP, 1985). Nigerian children, for instance, will say that they speak 'African'; Gujarati children claim to speak 'Indian'; and Panjabi-speaking Moslems report that they use 'Pakistani'. The choice of these terms suggests that children have drawn a number of conclusions about attitudes to their languages. First, there is widespread ignorance about the extent of linguistic diversity, whether in Africa or Asia: many teachers have simply never heard of the languages which their children speak. Secondly, when no attempt is made to find out about their backgrounds, it is natural for children to assume that their languages are of little interest to their teachers.

The extent of linguistic diversity experienced by many children is far beyond the experience of most monolinguals. Take the case of a Gujarati child whose first language is Kachi but who will also understand standard Gujarati. Through exposure to ever-popular videos, she will be familiar with Hindi and, while attending religious ceremonies in temples, she will hear Sanskrit or Bhojpuri, the langauge of the Ramayana. If her family has come via East Africa, she may hear Swahili. English will also be used, particularly in conversation with her siblings.

When schools are indifferent or even hostile to diversity, it is not surprising that children deny they are bilingual. Yet they are happy to discuss their skills in conversation with adults who show they value other languages. Children at the Project schools were open about the benefits of being able to speak to parents and other members of their family. They also clearly enjoyed having a secret language. As fifteen-year-old Vincent pointed out, the ability to speak Chinese is an asset 'if you want to talk to someone and you don't want anyone else to understand.' Children also talked about the benefits of being able to read and write another language, including keeping in touch through letters and making books.

During our visits to schools, it was clear that monolingual children, too, recognized

the benefits of bilingualism, although they were possibly less enthusiastic than their bilingual peers. For instance, they sometimes viewed European languages more favourably than non-European ones. In answer to the question, 'Do you think it's useful to be able to speak other languages?' one seven-year-old pointed at a book in Urdu and replied, 'Yes, but not this one!'

Discussions with even very young children reveal a wealth of information about attitudes and emerging theories of language. Another seven-year-old monolingual child speculated at length on the benefits of speaking other languages, placing his arguments very clearly within the context of his own experience:

> It's useful to read and write in other languages because if you were an adult and you didn't learn another language at school and you were taking someone to the hospital and it said 'Hospital', you wouldn't understand it would you? And if you wanted icecream and it said 'Icecream shop' you wouldn't know. It's helpful to read and write because instead of saying something you could write things, or if you can't write you can speak.

Teachers have a responsibility to encourage discussion and speculation of this kind. They also have a responsibility to present linguistic diversity both as a personal asset and as a resource for sharing. In schools where such practice is the norm, children don't need to pretend they only speak English.

'The parents in my class only want their children to learn English'

Parents are not a homogeneous group and there are many different ideas on which language(s) should be transmitted from one generation to the next, and how. It would be wrong to assume that children will speak English as a second language simply because they come from a linguistic minority background: many families make a decision to use English as the language of the home. Nor can we assume that children will necessarily want to learn the language of their parents and grandparents.

All the same, there is also a substantial body of evidence which shows that languages in addition to English are widely used in many ethnic minority homes (LMP, 1985; Alladina & Edwards, 1991). Children interviewed as part of the Project confirmed the same patterns of language use reported elsewhere: parents and older relatives usually speak the home language(s) among themselves and to their children; many can also read and write in the community or heritage language(s). Most children speak to their parents and elders either in English or in the home language; English is usually preferred in conversations with siblings and peers. While there is evidence of a shift to English, children none the less have extensive exposure to other languages. It is also a matter of record that very large numbers of families from many different speech communities send their children to classes in community or heritage languages both inside and outside mainstream schools (see LMP, 1985; Cummins & Danesi, 1990).

The community schools we visited as part of our research were good examples of the level of interest and commitment among parents and children. The Hounslow Chinese School, for instance, meets in a local primary school on Saturdays between 10.30 and 12.30. A headteacher, sixteen class teachers, three relief teachers and a librarian work with 285 children between the ages of five and sixteen, organized according to age and ability.

The school has a social as well as an educational function. Many of the children come from quite long distances and so the school becomes a meeting place for families. Parents contribute in a number of ways: by helping to supervise playtime; by forming part of a rota on call if children feel ill or have accidents; by fundraising; and, in the case of one parent we spoke to, by babysitting for one of the teachers. The atmosphere is welcoming and lively.

The Ramgarhia Sabha Sunday School is another thriving community enterprise. The school started in the early 1980s in a room at the Sikh temple, or gurdwara, where families gathered to listen to stories. The classes now meet at the local primary school and cater for 350 students between the ages of five and eighteen, organized according to age and ability. Each teacher has a parent or past student to support their work in class. Three of the twenty-four teachers are responsible for administration and stand in for absent colleagues. Some teachers also work in mainstream schools, but many do not. Attempts are under way to devise a syllabus, build up resources and offer guidelines on classroom management.

Classes are held between 11am and 1pm. The two-hour session is divided equally into Panjabi language teaching and Sikh studies. Although these are seen as two separate functions of the Sunday school, there tends to be an overlap, especially with the younger classes. The school organizes a range of educational trips and children contribute to religious and cultural events at the gurdwara.

Teachers in community school settings such as these clearly need no persuasion about the value of bilingualism. Many teachers in mainstream schools have also begun to realize the cognitive and social benefits of speaking other languages. The research evidence (for an overview see, for example, Baker, 1993) points clearly to the importance of developing children's first language, not only in speech but in reading and writing. Literacy skills developed in one language are readily transferred to second and subsequent languages.

Many teachers in the Project schools felt

passionately about the importance of allowing children to develop their home language alongside English. Teachers in Thomas Buxton Junior School, for instance, spoke enthusiastically about a boy who had gone back to Bangladesh for a year. On returning to London, he was totally literate in Bengali, impressing everyone with his ability to operate effectively in both languages. One teacher argued that the time he spent in Bangladesh had 'enriched his English.' As the headteacher commented: 'In an ideal world, if we had two teachers in each class, one English and one Bengali, then the children would have amazing results'.

Recent theories on the cognitive benefits of bilingualism are, of course, unfamiliar to most parents. Several teachers in the Project schools talked of their responsibility to explain why they were working in this way, since parents often feel that time spent on the home language is to the detriment of children's development in English.

'The parents never turn up for school events'

Many teachers feel very discouraged by the fact that minority parents often fail to keep appointments to talk about their children's progress in school, or support their children by attending social events. All too often, this behaviour is interpreted as a lack of interest. Yet, when schools address this question from the parents' perspective, a very different picture emerges.

Schooling in Pakistan or Somalia or Hong Kong is likely to have been a very different experience from school in the new country. Teaching methods will have been a great deal more formal and teachers are invested with sole responsibility for children's learning. The expectation that parents should be involved in a dialogue with teachers about their children's education can seem strange and intimidating. So can formal letters inviting parents to events at school.

Sometimes this kind of problem has been resolved quite simply. By offering both early afternoon and evening appointments on two or three different days, shift workers may find it easier to attend (see, for instance, Kenway, 1994). The knowledge that an interpreter will be present may transform what would otherwise be a stressful meeting for parents who lack confidence in speaking English.

Staging different kinds of social events may also help to break the ice. While middle-class white parents may feel at ease in cheese and wine evenings, other kinds of social gathering may prove less intimidating to a wider range of parents. International evenings where parents can enjoy a range of food, music and dance can be a step in the right direction, though these will never work unless other aspects of school life demonstrate a serious commitment to diversity. Parents are also far more likely to join in when asked directly by the teacher than when they receive letters sent home with children.

'We would never be able to get the parents in our school to help in class'

Schools often start to address the challenge of involving parents by rearranging parents' evenings or staging some kind of international event. Sometimes they are disappointed with the results and fail to recognize fundamental organizational obstacles to good home–school relations. When all the non-verbal signs tell parents, 'Stay out, this is our territory,' it is hardly surprising that invitations to parents' events have a disappointing response. Until parents feel welcome, little progress can be made.

The visual environment in schools

The visual environment in schools can also send powerful messages to parents. As part of our fieldwork in the Project schools we photographed the surroundings in which teachers and children worked.

Signs

Signs are essential in providing information and directing people around the building. If a school population has parents and children who speak other languages, multilingual signs are needed to communicate effectively and provide a welcoming atmosphere. Many of the multilingual signs in schools are produced commercially. Signs made by parents and teachers are a cheaper alternative which can still effectively convey the message. Even when a school has commercially produced signs in its main corridors, home-made additions can be found in many classrooms.

Labels & nameplates

Children's nameplates in different scripts can be used to mark objects in the school such as coat hooks, trays, books. Labels in other languages and scripts can also be used to identify the contents of different boxes or different areas of the classroom, and to caption children's work displayed on walls and boards. Alphabet and number charts are another way to introduce the notion of different writing and numbering systems.

Displays

Teachers can involve children in creating classroom displays. These can serve as a focus for projects and are another way of presenting visual aspects of different languages and cultures.

Artefacts

Many classrooms keep a stock of artefacts associated with different cultures, such as cooking utensils, food packets, clothes, musical instruments and writing implements.

Posters & notices

As well as making bright and interesting wall areas, posters offer opportunities to include writing, images and patterns from a range of different cultures. As with signs, they can be commercially produced or made by teachers and children within the school.

School organization

Access

Easy access to teaching staff is an extremely important first step in making parents feel comfortable in a school. In Redlands, a primary school in southern England, some twenty-eight different languages are spoken (Edwards & Redfern, 1988). The headteacher stands at the entrance to the school when the bell rings in the morning. She keeps the first fifteen minutes of the day free so that she can deal with urgent problems – parents don't need to wait for an appointment. Teachers have an open classroom policy. Parents don't leave their children at the school gates or even at the classroom door. Instead there is an expectation that they come into the classroom at the start or end of school, to share information about what has happened at home, or to admire the children's work for the day. Once a week in the first two years of school, parents are invited to come and work alongside their children for part of the morning. Initiatives of this kind pay rich rewards. For many years, attendance at parents' evenings has been close to 100 per cent; and there is no shortage of parent volunteers for a wide range of social and educational events.

Workshops

Another way of involving parents is through workshops. Sometimes parents use these sessions to produce books in the community language for their children to read, or to provide translations of stories which their children have written in English. On other occasions teachers use the sessions to focus on a particular area of the curriculum such as maths or reading. This was the case in Thomas Buxton Junior School:

We have a session to show parents how we teach maths. It's a practical workshop in the hall from 10am to 12. We write to all the parents about it and involve some children from each class. They make games. There's a cooking session going on – measurement, etc. We prepare worksheets for parents to try out. They just come and try things out with us. It's mostly the children who help and explain what to do.

Written communication

If a school is serious about involving parents in their children's education, all the important documents – school brochures, policy statements, information booklets – need to be made available in all the languages of the school. In most cases, the responsibility for co-ordinating these efforts falls on monolingual headteachers or principals. There is a variety of solutions. Most local education authorities and school boards offer a translation service; in some schools, bilingual teachers are given time outside the classroom to do this work; on other occasions parents are happy to perform this role. Ephemeral communications such as newsletters pose more pressing problems. In a school where dozens of different languages are spoken, it is clearly not possible to translate every letter home into all the languages. In these cases, the only possible solution is to provide translations into the major languages of the school. Even this requires good organization. All the relevant information needs to be gathered several days in advance of the proposed 'mailing' date to allow sufficient time for translation.

The use of other languages in written communications with parents sends important messages. However, we also need to remember that other cultures place greater emphasis on oral communication. Teachers need to step outside the school gates and make use of local

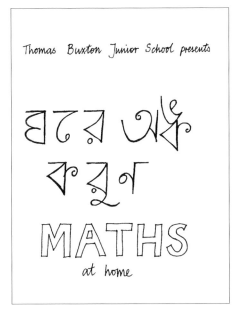

Thomas Buxton Junior School presents

ঘরে অঙ্ক করুণ

MATHS

at home

Figure 2.1 Front cover of 'Maths at home', a booklet written in Bengali and English to explain how parents can help with maths

networks. Who are the important figures in the communities served by the school? And where do people meet informally? In schools with an open classroom policy, teachers can issue personal invitations to parents. Home visits are another useful way of establishing trusting relationships. And, while British teachers tend to be hesitant about speaking to parents on the phone, North American teachers find this an effective way of making contact with parents who don't accompany their children to school.

Developing a whole school policy

Linguistic minority parents – and teachers – make it clear that they welcome attempts to reflect the broader community in the schools. As one Panjabi teacher explained:

> Displaying our work makes our own culture and religion more important and of equal value with things like Christmas and Easter … [it brings] diversity into our children's growing up.

Developments such as open classrooms, flexible consultation, the provision of interpreters and translation, workshops and attention to the visual environment are essential in establishing good and trusting relationships with parents. In effective schools, practical initiatives of this kind are often formalized in policy documents developed by the staff.

It is important that policy documents also show an awareness of the wider social reality for ethnic minority children. Issues which are frequently addressed include:

- *Racial harassment* What steps must a school take to prevent racist name-calling and other forms of racist abuse?
- *Role models* To what extent is the population which the school serves reflected in the staff? Are ethnic minority staff reserved to ancillary roles or are they well represented throughout the school?
- *Ethnic monitoring* What steps are being taken to ensure that the performance of different ethnic groups – and girls and boys – is being adequately monitored and what

measures are necessary when there is evidence that a particular group is underperforming?

Time invested in creating the right ethos will be amply rewarded with an enthusiastic response – from monolingual and bilingual children – to opportunities for reading, writing, speaking and listening to other languages.

Summary

Getting off on the right foot

Many parents feel uncomfortable about approaching schools and teachers. Sometimes this is because of their own very different experience of education. Sometimes it is because schools seem intimidating. Schools can create a more welcoming atmosphere by:

- acknowledging linguistic and cultural diversity in the visual environment of the school and the curriculum offered to the children
- allowing parents open access to classrooms at the start and close of every day
- looking closely at the timing of parents' evenings and other school events
- ensuring that an interpreter is present whenever necessary
- translating school documents
- involving all staff in developing an equal opportunities policy and discussing this openly with parents.

3 Resources for speaking and listening

Speaking more than one language

In the early years of the twentieth century, children in many different countries were being physically punished for speaking their home languages in school. Yet, by the late 1970s, many teachers were beginning to explore creative ways of incorporating different languages into the classroom. Some teachers still believe that their sole responsibility is to teach children to speak English and that the best way to achieve this end is to exclude all other languages. Various developments, including the campaign for English only in the USA and the introduction of a national curriculum in the UK, with a strong emphasis on standard English, have helped to reinforce this view.

However, research evidence and language support teachers' experience in mainstream classrooms point firmly in the opposite direction. There is a growing understanding that a sound foundation in the first language is essential for good progress in second and subsequent language learning (Cummins, 1994). There is also a much better appreciation of the links between language and identity: children whose languages are valued and respected will feel more confident and secure than children whose languages are ignored or treated with contempt.

Life with more than one language is complex. For instance, the experience of parents and children in many minority communities is often multilingual rather than bilingual. The 'language of the home' or 'the first language' co-exists not only with English but with the language used for wider communication in the country of origin. Take the case of the Sikh and Moslem children at Havelock Primary School. For Sikh children, Panjabi is both the language of the home and the language of religion and culture. The Guru Granth Sahib, the holy book of the Sikhs, is written in Panjabi using the Gurmukhi script. Moslem children from neighbouring Pakistan also speak a dialect of Panjabi at home. In mosque classes, however, the Qur'ān and other religious texts are written in Urdu using a Perso-Arabic script known as Nastaliq. Urdu is closely related to both Panjabi and Hindi, but makes extensive use of vocabulary derived from Persian.

Similarly, the majority of children at Thomas Buxton Junior School come from a region of Bangladesh known as Sylhet. At home they speak Sylheti, a largely unwritten language, rather than Bengali, the official language of Bangladesh. Many Bangladeshi children study both Bengali, the language of literature and learning, and Arabic, the language of their religion, in classes outside school.

It is not always clear which language(s) teachers should encourage. The answer is likely to vary according to the speech community in question and also the settings in which minority languages are used. Whereas bilingual teachers will almost certainly use the language of the home to communicate with children in the classroom, community – or heritage – language teachers wi'   h ә language of the wider ethnolinguistic community, but will also draw in varying degrees on the language of the home.

Attempts to support children's use of more than one language are varied. In the USA, Canada and Wales, bilingual education programmes are now widespread, giving children the opportunity to develop spoken and written skills in two languages. In New Zealand, the kohanga reo (or language nest) movement ensures that increasing numbers of children can learn through English and Maori. In British schools with large numbers of bilingual pupils – especially where there is a high proportion of one language group – bilingual support teachers working alongside the class teacher use a variety of strategies to help children develop both English and the home language.

All the mainstream Project schools had high proportions of bilingual children and employed bilingual support teachers. Thomas Buxton Junior School in east London, for instance, had 290 children on roll during fieldwork, ninety-eight per cent of whom were Sylheti speakers whose families came originally from Bangladesh. There was a small number of Urdu- and Panjabi-speaking pupils and just one monolingual English child. Out of a staff of twenty, three class teachers and two ancillary staff spoke Bengali. The school was very supportive of bilingualism and both staff and children felt comfortable about switching between Sylheti and English, according to topic or audience. Teachers talked in terms of using Sylheti 'to make things clear' and 'using their discretion' about the best ways to put their bilingual skills to work.

A second Project school, Havelock Primary in west London, worked in similar ways. Here sixty-nine per cent of the children were Indian Sikhs and twenty-five per cent were Pakistani Moslems; all of these children spoke mutually intelligible dialects of Panjabi at home. Five of the class teachers and two nursery nurses spoke Urdu or Panjabi. One teacher explained that she uses the children's home language 'quite spontaneously, whenever it seems right.' Another commented that she uses 'whatever language is best to express what we want to say.' Here, too, children feel free to use their home languages in the classroom.

In schools where the proportion of bilingual children is smaller, or where the population is more linguistically diverse, approaches tend to be different. In Redlands Primary, for instance, thirty per cent of the children are bilingual and, between them, speak some twenty-eight different languages. The wider spread of languages means that, although teachers actively encourage children to use their home languages, most children choose to use English in most situations. None the less, children are able to speak and hear their home languages in a range of different situations: welcoming parents and others at social events; answering the register; singing and reading in various school performances. There is a lunchtime Urdu club and the younger children regularly listen to stories told in parallel by an English-speaking teacher and an Urdu-speaking nursery nurse.

Acknowledging diversity

Teachers who want to promote bilingualism need to be well-informed about the linguistic background of their students. They need to know, for instance, that children from the Indian sub-continent speak a very wide variety of languages, not 'Indian' or 'Pakistani'. They need to understand that, in some communities, one variety is spoken in the home and another is used in education and yet another for religious purposes. Thus most Pakistani children in Britain will speak

Panjabi at home, but study Urdu in community classes.

Teachers also have a responsibility to pronounce names as accurately as possible and to understand that, in different societies, naming practices can be very different. For instance, in most Moslem families, each member has a different last name. Males are given a personal name (eg Hafiz, Habib) which is used only by the family and close friends, and a religious name (eg Mohammed, Hussein) normally used in conjunction with the personal name. Sometimes the personal name comes first, sometimes the religious name. Acquaintances will normally use the 'calling name' which consists of the religious and personal name. Some men also have hereditary names such as Quereshi and Choudry which they use as family names. Formally we might refer to Mr Mohammed Khalid Quereshi, informally to Mohammed Khalid.

Moslem women, in contrast, are given first and second names. The first name (eg Fozia, Aneel) is personal; the second is either a female title (eg Begum, Bibi) or a second personal name (eg Akhtar, Jan). The second name can act as the family name or, alternatively, the husband's last name is adopted on marriage. Thus when Fatma Bibi marries Mohammed Aslam, she may remain Fatma Bibi or change to Fatma (Bibi) Aslam. The correct form of address will be Fatma Bibi and not Mrs Bibi, which is roughly equivalent to being called Mrs Mrs. Moslem settlers often adapt to the naming practices in their new country, so there may be still further variations.

Promoting speaking and listening in other languages

A wide variety of activities lend themselves to a multilingual approach: group discussion; storytelling; drama, role play, and puppetry. Recent technologies also offer exciting new possibilities for the production and use of multilingual audio and video resources.

Group work and discussion

Group work is an effective way to encourage children to speak and listen in other languages, although the arrangement of the groups needs to be flexible. Just as it is often more effective to start exploring gender-related questions in single-sex groups, there are many issues which are best explored in groups arranged according to shared language. Thus children and young people discussing different aspects of family life or moral culture may find reassurance in the support of a group of peers with similar experiences. If the aim is to allow children to explore ideas and feelings, they will probably use the language associated with these experiences. Children may switch between English and the language of the home, depending on the situation and the other speakers.

Bilingual storytelling

Stories can be read or told. When teachers use a book, they can draw on one of a number of approaches (see, for instance, Martin-Jones *et al.*, 1992). They can read first in one language, then in the next. Alternatively, each page can be read in both languages. The second language can be read as it stands, or retold in a style adapted to the particular needs of the audience. Bilingual teachers can read both versions of the story. Monolingual teachers need the help of bilingual teachers or parents.

Stories do not, of course, depend on books. Professional storytellers – in English and in other languages – are in ever-increasing demand. For mixed audiences, most bilingual storytellers usually either tell traditional stories in English or switch between English and another language, allowing listeners to use actions, mimes, facial expressions and tone of voice, as well as the interspersed English, to work out the meaning of the other language. However, storytellers such as Roop Singh sometimes perform entirely in the community language, even with monolingual English-speaking audiences. He was once asked: 'Why stories in Panjabi to non-Panjabi speakers?' In reply, he goes back some years:

> A teacher in a middle-class all-white school asked for something new and exciting, so I decided to tell them the story of Jack and the Beanstalk in Punjabi. It was

one of the most successful sessions I've ever had. They couldn't understand what I was saying, but they could grasp what was going on – they could pick up the vibes.
(O'Grady, 1994, p. 4)

Drama and role play

Drama and role play in other languages can also encourage the use of other languages. A number of 'theatre in education' companies now specialize in bilingual drama. *Kola Pata Bhut* (*The hopscotch ghost*), a production by the London-based Half Moon Young People's Theatre, is a good example of how other languages can be integrated very naturally into performance (Fitzgerald, 1993). The four main characters move fluidly between English, Bengali and Sylheti, but language differences are soon forgotten as the audience is taken up with the story.

Bilingual drama need not be limited to professional or semi-professional performers. By using children's everyday skills as interpreters, it is possible for them to act out their daily multilingual reality and, at the same time, allow their monolingual peers access to their world. Take the scenario where an English-speaking child visits the home of a Panjabi-speaking friend. The conversation with parents and grandparents is likely to take place in Panjabi, but the bilingual child will offer summaries and explanations in English. The same pattern applies to many other situations, such as visits to the doctor or parents' evenings at school.

Case study: Practical parent power

The following is adapted from *Working with parents* by Penny Kenway (1994) and describes part of a project to involve parents with children's reading and literacy.

Activities in the nursery at Wellington Primary School in west London provide a good example of parental involvement in children's language and literacy activities. A letter, translated into seven community languages, was sent to all parents inviting them to attend a series of workshops in which their skills and expertise could be used to make things for the children to use in their language work.

The first workshop was used to make hand and finger puppets for extending language. Teachers felt that this was a topic that would attract parents whose lack of confidence in English might inhibit them from attending other workshops. They also felt that it was a good way to increase the selection of puppets in the nursery and to explain to parents the value of puppets in storytelling and role play and the opportunities they offer for children to extend their language.

Another of the early workshops focussed on making games to encourage reading development. Parents used multiple copies of photos of the children to make games such as Snap and Pairs. One of the advantages of such games is that they can be played in English or any other language.

The workshop was an undoubted success. Mothers who had not previously been involved – perhaps because of their English – felt confident about coming into the nursery and using their expertise in sewing to make puppets for the children.

Audio-visual resources

The most important resources for developing speaking and listening skills are clearly people who speak other languages. However, the use of audio-visual material also deserves attention.

Several British publishers produce tape and story packs: dual language story books, most often in English and Bengali, Gujarati, Panjabi or Urdu, accompanied by a tape which uses one side for the English reading and the other for a second language version. In the USA, there is a wide selection of Spanish audio cassettes for children aimed at the large Hispanic population. Commercially produced tapes can be usefully supplemented by tapes produced in schools by parents, children and bilingual members of staff.

Videos and films in other languages are also an important part of many children's experiences. Various courses for young children in a range of European languages are widely available and some companies are also starting to produce videos of stories in non-European languages. Educational Media and Film, for instance, produce the *Pick a story, choose a language* videos, each of which tells five well-known children's stories in English, Bengali, Turkish or Gujarati.

Multi-media packs, too, are likely to become important as classroom learning resources (Abbott, 1994a; Routh, 1994). CD-ROM is creating many new opportunities for listening to other languages. The storage capabilities of this medium mean that it will be feasible for stories to be offered in not only a range of different languages, but also different dialects or accents in the same software package. The first multilingual CD-ROMs for children have already appeared. *Just Grandma and me* (Living Books, 1992), for instance, can be used in English, Japanese and Spanish. Many teachers and parents await further developments in this area with considerable interest.

The most widely used listening resource in the Project schools was audio cassettes. Teachers stressed the need for well-produced tapes that would appeal to a wide range of interests, and for a well-organized listening area with good storage facilities and good cataloguing for easy access. They were keen to encourage children to use the tapes in a variety of ways (individually or in small groups) and for a variety of purposes (for entertainment, for finding information, or for following instructions).

Audio cassettes also offer children and parents a range of creative possibilities: telling or reading their own stories on to tape; acting out dialogues and dramas; performing songs, lullabies and rhymes; recording interviews which can be transcribed later. All of these activities can take place in any language and form an important part of the class or school resource collection.

One Project school, Thomas Buxton Junior, has given very careful attention to the use and creation of tapes. Teachers use a checklist of points to consider when producing audio cassettes including audience and purpose; format (for example, Bengali on one side, English on the other); story reading or telling with questions or tasks at the end; presentation (one person reading, or drama with more than one person or voice); and organization (checking for accuracy, cataloguing). They also have a list of suggestions for looking after and using cassettes in the classroom covering storage, record keeping, ways of encouraging children both to listen (whole class, small groups, individual children) and to make cassettes (for example, 'radio' programmes for each other).

Summary

Speaking and listening: strategies and resources

The speaking and listening skills of bilingual children are often more advanced than their literacy development. Encouragement of these skills provides an excellent basis for future language development in both English and community languages. It also sends clear messages to both bilingual and monolingual children that linguistic diversity is a valuable resource.

This chapter has suggested ways in which teachers can encourage children to make use of their bilingual skills by:
- being well-informed about which languages children speak, with whom and when
- showing respect for other naming practices and pronouncing children's names correctly
- creating opportunities for the use of other languages in group work, discussion, storytelling, drama and role play
- involving parents and other bilingual adults in classroom activities creating and using audio-visual materials.

4 Resources for reading

Literacies in English-speaking classrooms

Our understanding of different approaches to the written word has undergone a dramatic transformation in recent years. The traditional assumption was that learning to read was simply a matter of acquiring and applying a set of sub-skills. Today, writers such as Barton (1994) and Street (1993) have begun to talk of 'literacies' instead of 'literacy', in recognition of the very social nature of our relationship with print and the ways in which this relationship is negotiated very differently by different groups of people.

In this part of the book, we will be looking at the range of experiences which many children bring with them to English-speaking classrooms and the implications of differences for their performance in school. We then move on to look at the ways in which books in other languages acknowledge and extend bilingual children's experience of literacy; and the various design and status issues which they present.

'Maktab' literacy

The Moslem experience of literacy is an excellent example of how the same phenomenon is approached in culturally different ways. In traditional Moslem religious schools or 'maktabs', children learn, among other things, to recite by heart whole passages of the Qur'ān. Maktabs have definite boundaries between 'work' and 'play' which make them very different from mainstream schools. The same principles often spill over from Qur'ānic to voluntary community language classes including Urdu, Bengali and Gujarati. Children questioned in a study by Gregory (1993), for instance, were clear that they 'read and write' in Bengali school and 'play' in English school. In classes which often last for two hours without a break, children remain seated on the floor or at the table and all talk is directed to the task in hand. The typical sequence is demonstration, repeat, practice and then test. Tuition is exact and direct. The child answers and will be told either, 'Yes' or 'Not like that, like this'.

The skills which children need for reading the Qur'ān are very different from those required in school. Street (1984), for instance, argues that maktab literacy often produces children who recognize passages they have memorized by their position on the page, layout and style rather than by 'cracking the phonemic code'.

Yet, despite the differences between maktab and school literacy, Moslem children acquire many skills in mosque classes which are useful when they learn to read in English. They have, for instance, a sound understanding of the links between speech and writing. For readers of Latin scripts, words are bounded on either side by spaces. Arabic script uses different forms of the same letter for the beginning, middle and end of words. These – and not spaces – help the reader break up the stream of print on the page. Although the two writing systems are different, children with experience of maktab literacy have a well-developed sense of what constitutes a word.

Maktab literacy also develops an understanding of different formats and conventions for printed text. Children not only learn that Arabic script goes from right to left and top to bottom of the page, but that the page can be broken up in different ways: words in the margin may be a commentary on the main text; blocks of print may be set at different angles or across the corners of the page. Although conventions may differ between writing systems, an awareness of different textual arrangements is very useful in learning to read English.

Finally, maktab literacy helps develop skills for non-sequential reading. In order to find specific passages to justify an argument, students learn to thumb their way around the Qur'ān and other texts using, for example, headings and contents pages.

Literacy in the Chinese community

The Chinese approach to the written word shares many similarities with maktab literacy. Much importance is attached to the values of Confucianism which include respect for parents and achievement in education. There is a strict division between work and play. Children sit in rows and do as the teacher directs them. Children practise characters over and over until they are perfect. If they forget or misplace a single stroke, they may completely change the meaning, so close attention to detail is essential. As in the maktab, children who attend Chinese community classes recite words in chorus after the teacher. They learn through repetition, memorization and careful copying.

Chinese characters offer no clues as to their pronunciation. They are ideographs or symbols which work in a similar way to numbers in European languages. Thus '7' represents seven, sept, siete, saith, etc. Similarly, the same character is pronounced as 'hok' in Cantonese, 'xue' in Putonghua (or Mandarin) and 'hak' in Hokkien. Although there are various systems for the romanisation of a number of varieties, the Chinese abroad still maintain traditional writing (see Sampson, 1985 for a full discussion).

Wang (1973) estimates that, in order to read a Chinese newspaper, you need to know between 4,000 and 7,000 characters. Wong (1991) talks of the particular difficulties which this raises for children whose contact with the written word is, for the most part, limited to weekend community schools. Inevitably they quickly forget the characters introduced in class. To help them remember the pronunciation, they often write transliterations alongside the English text as the teacher reads to them.

Literacy is a high status pursuit within the Chinese community. Books are held in very high esteem and parents believe that children must prove themselves worthy through hard work. In much the same way that Moslem children are given the Qur'ān when they have worked their way through Arabic primers, many Chinese children are rewarded with books only when they have learned to read.

Dispelling the myths

Because many teachers have only been exposed to one kind of literacy, they tend to assume that theirs is the 'right' approach and are unaware of the different experiences which children bring with them to school. Assumptions about what counts as a supportive learning environment are often simplistic. Many people assume, for instance, that only children from middle-class families have very wide exposure to reading. Yet literacy is an integral part of every home: official forms, junk mail and free newspapers come flooding into every house; the omnipresent television offers many interesting encounters with written language; shopping lists, calendars, phone books, messages and greetings cards all form part of everyday life.

It is often believed that minority children's experience of literacy is particularly impoverished. The findings of a research project in the East London boroughs of Newham and Tower Hamlets (Gregory, 1993) point to a different reality. The plight of the Bangladeshi community in this area has given rise to some concern in recent years: unemployment is high, racist attacks are frequent and educational underachievement is widespread. Limited experience of literacy, however, is not a plausible explanation for underachievement.

East London has many bookshops selling the Qur'ān and poetry books, autobiographies, newspapers and children's books in Bengali. Most grocery shops also sell children's primers for learning to read Bengali. These books are displayed in a bookcase in the homes of the children in the project while reading primers, exercise books, pencils and often a special school-bag are kept away from younger children, usually out of sight in a high cupboard.

The children spend an average of eleven hours a week in literacy classes outside mainstream schooling. Most go to Bengali classes between 5pm and 7pm three times a week; they spend a similar amount of time in Mosque classes where they learn to read classical Arabic. Some children receive one-to-one tuition; others attend classes in private homes or in community centres. In all cases, parents who often have very limited means are making a financial investment in their children's education. The notion that literacy is not valued or that children have only limited exposure to the written word clearly has no foundation.

There is no simple equation between exposure to print and success in reading. Urzúa (1986) makes this point very clearly in a comparison of three Cambodian refugee families in the USA. In Vuong's home, there was no shortage of reading materials: bus schedules, tide charts for the family's fishing trips, maps and calendars, newspapers, brochures and newsletters. Vuong's father spoke French, Laotian, English and Thai as well as his native Cambodian, and Khymer–English and French–English dictionaries were clearly on display. Literature from the Buddhist Society in Cambodian, and from the Khymer Liberation Front, in both English and Cambodian, was scattered everywhere. In contrast, Cham and Sonkla lived with their widowed mothers in apartments where there was very little evidence of reading material. The only visible materials in Cambodian were calendars and a couple of letters from relatives; the only visible materials in English were the phone book and books from school in a small bookcase.

Those who stress the value of children's early literacy experiences might expect Vuong to have made much more rapid progress than Cham and Sonkla. This was not the case. Vuong was struggling with literacy; Cham and Sonkla were reading and writing enthusiastically.

Reading in many languages

Many of the children interviewed during the course of the Project talked not only about the reading materials they used in community classes, but of the newspaper and magazine articles which they read and the books which they borrowed from the local library. Calendars, shop signs, food labelling and other forms of environmental print are also part of their everyday experience.

Children learn to read other languages in a variety of settings: in community schools, with private tutors, with their parents or older siblings in the home. Their levels of proficiency also vary a great deal. Children who have recently arrived often read with confidence in their community languages. Most of the children we talked to, however, had been born in England and, although they experienced few problems with the spoken language, often complained that reading and writing were very difficult. Some Pakistani children, for instance, explained that they found it difficult to tell where words in Urdu end. There was a general consensus, though, that things get easier. A sixteen-year-old student in the Chinese school pointed out:

> Reading involves a good memory really because once you pick a word up and you keep on repeating it, it just locks into your mind. Somebody who hasn't done it before won't be able to understand a very simple word, but it's just natural for us.

How can schools build on these varied experiences? Where bilingual adults – teachers, parents and non-teaching assistants – are available, it is possible to provide support for children's reading as a normal part of the school day. Monolingual teachers can help by ensuring a plentiful supply of reading materials in other languages. These can take many different forms. Earlier in the book we looked at various aspects of the visual environment of

schools: signs, posters, children's nameplates, alphabet and number charts. Teachers can stock school libraries and classrooms with books in a startling array of languages, produced locally or imported from other countries. In some cases, these are single language editions; in others, they are dual language books in which English appears in conjunction with a second language.

Multilingual resources raise many interesting questions for teachers and designers. Some are peculiar to single language texts; others affect only dual language books. We will also be looking at translation, an issue which is relevant for both single language editions of the same book and dual language books. What problems present themselves? And how can we ensure high standards?

Figure 4.1 Page from *The snowman* by Raymond Briggs.
London: Puffin Books, 1980

An example of a wordless picture book.

Books in other languages

Books in other languages are an important
element in the resourcing of multilingual
classrooms. The presence of these books sends
clear messages about the status which schools
and teachers attach to other languages. Many
recently arrived children react as if they have
discovered a long lost friend. For instance,
Grace Feuerverger (1994, p. 133) reports an
incident in a Toronto school in which the
teacher-librarian presented a Farsi book to
an Iranian student:

> The child's eyes lit up and he asked, 'Is
> that Farsi?' and I said, 'Yes, do you want
> it?' and he just looked spellbound. And
> then another Iranian boy who's been here
> for a while became his reading 'buddy'
> and they read together.

While many monolingual English-speaking
teachers show a marked preference for the
dual language books which form the focus for
the next section, bilingual teachers tend to
stress the advantages of single language books.
These teachers often work in community
school settings where the emphasis is on helping children to become biliterate. Many bilingual teachers argue that, when faced with dual
language texts, children would gravitate
towards the English and be less motivated to
try to read the other language text. We return
to this theme in greater detail on pages 54–55.

It seems appropriate at this point to men-
tion wordless picture books, an important
new genre in children's literature. They allow
beginners to tell the story as they see it, and to
develop an understanding of fundamental
features such as sequence and climax as they
go (Figure 4.1). They are ideal for 'reading' in
any language. Children can use the books
independently, share the telling with other
children or 'read' to bilingual adults, at home
and in school, secure in the knowledge that
their version of the story is as valid as any
written text.

Books for children are available in a large number of languages other than English and come from a variety of different sources, including mainstream publishers, community publishers, suppliers of imported books and subsidized publishing projects.

Mainstream publishers

Various mainstream UK publishers, no doubt influenced by the national curriculum for modern foreign languages, have begun to realize the potential of children's books in the languages of the European Union, especially French, German, Spanish and Italian. These books appeal to two main audiences: the small number of children who speak these languages; and parents anxious that their children should acquire a foreign language. Books in other languages produced by mainstream publishers tend to work better for children who are already bilingual than for language learners. They are usually written in naturalistic language which is well beyond the competence of beginners. There are, however, notable exceptions. The text in Figure 4.2 uses simple, repetitive structures easily accessible to language learners; and the illustrations provide good visual clues to the meaning.

In the USA, growing numbers of books in Spanish aim to meet the needs of the large Hispanic population. These include books for emergent readers and whole language programmes, big and small books for shared reading and information books. American publishers are also beginning to produce small numbers of titles in languages such as Chinese, Korean, Vietnamese and Haitian.

lento come una lumaca,   piccolo come una formica,

Figure 4.2 Double page spread from *Veloce come un grillo* by Audrey Wood, illustrated by Don Wood, Italian translation by Somona Artandidi. Ristampa: Child's Play (International) Ltd, 1982

An example of a book in Italian which uses simple repetitive linguistic structures and illustrations to provide clues to meaning.

Community publishers

These tend to be small enterprises, more motivated by the desire to help maintain minority languages than by the desire to make a profit. Although most community publishers specialize in dual language books, some also produce small numbers of single language titles. These books are produced to standards similar to those of mainstream publishers, using good-quality paper, full-colour photographs and illustrations, and professional typesetting. Print runs for any given language are small and production costs are high: it is often only possible to produce a large range of languages by using the same illustrations and changing the language on each print run.

Figure 4.3 Examples of books from India at the Darpan Bengali School.

Imported books

Many books in languages other than English are imported from countries like India which have a long and thriving publishing tradition (Figure 4.3). Publishers like the New Delhi Children's Book Trust have served as a valuable platform for many children's writers and authors, and specialist booksellers such as Soma Books and Books from India in London have done much valuable work in disseminating their books.

Throughout the world, books from Taiwan, Hong Kong and the Republic of China are widely available in shops in the various Chinatowns. In the UK, most community schools use books supplied by the Hong Kong Government Office in London. In the USA, community schools draw on a number of sources. For instance, the Department of Overseas Affairs of the Republic of China is the sole supplier of textbooks to community schools in San Francisco (Wong, 1992), while most schools in New York use books from Taiwan.

Teachers in the USA and the UK, however, are often very critical of these materials (Tsow, 1984; Fan, 1981), pointing to the same kinds of problems as those working in other linguistic minority communities. Concern is often expressed that imported books deal with experiences far removed from readers born outside the home country. A child who, with the exception of a few brief visits to the country of origin, has known only a western urban environment, may find it difficult to relate to the experiences and expectations of books conceived for a very different audience. It is possible to argue, however, that such a view is far too sweeping. Many Indian books for children deal with themes which have an international appeal. The repertoire of writers like Ira Saxena, for instance, extends to computer adventures and environmental issues.

Na'a ne fakasiosio he lalo
niu mo ne pehē,
" 'Oku malu nai eni?
'Ika'i, 'oku 'ikai."

Na'a ne fakasiosio ha loto
nge'esi kapa māpukupaku mo ne pehē,
" 'Oku malu nai eni?
'Ika'i, 'oku 'ikai."

Figure 4.4 Page from *Ko e feitu'u malu* by Sue Mooar. Wellington, New Zealand:
Ministry of Education, 1992

One of the books produced by subsidy from the New Zealand government. It has
full-colour illustrations and is well printed on good quality paper.

A second problem relates to differences in linguistic competence. The language level of children born abroad is usually several years behind the norm for the home country. As a result, texts within the reach of children overseas are often felt to be too babyish.

A final problem concerns appearance. Books produced in Hong Kong and Taiwan are usually of a similar look and feel to those produced in the English-speaking world and western Europe. Books from countries like India, Pakistan and Bangladesh, however, have a very different feel. This is particularly true of older books which make up a large proportion of other language resources in many schools. The paper used is often rough or very glossy. It also tends to be flimsy and 'show-through' from the page behind is a common feature. Printing quality can be different, too, resulting in either very bright or very faded colours. Illustrations can be stylistically unfamiliar to readers from another culture. These are all elements which contribute to the overall 'quality' of the book. This issue is discussed again on pages 49–51.

Subsidized publishing

Various indigenous languages receive government support for publishing. The Welsh Joint Education Committee set up a specialist panel of teachers, language advisers, college lecturers and librarians to vet all new books in Welsh and guarantees to purchase a copy of any approved title for every Welsh-medium school. In Scotland, the government-assisted Gaelic Books Council has considerably stimulated Gaelic publishing since the early 1960s. More recently, a consortium has formed Acair, a publishing house that specializes in educational material in Gaelic.

In Wales and Scotland, minority publishing is aimed at just one linguistic minority. In New Zealand the situation is more complex. The Ministry of Education Learning Media Department offers an excellent model for other language publishing, producing a very wide range of outstanding books in a range of languages including English, Cook Islands Maori, Samoan, Tuvaluan and Tongan (Figure 4.4).

In all these cases, however, there is a recognition that publishing in minority languages is not a commercial proposition. Any government committed to helping minority communities to maintain their mother tongues must be prepared to subsidize initiatives. Financial support is not restricted to materials for indigenous populations. Various governments have funded curriculum materials for the children of citizens overseas. The Italian government, for instance, has produced a course book for use in heritage language programmes in Canada; the Hong Kong government has funded the production of similar materials for use in Chinese community schools in Britain; and regional resources centres in the USA have developed bilingual teaching materials with the help of federal or state funds for the implementation of the 1968 Bilingual Education Act. These materials

我家在倫敦西區，步行到溫布敦地鐵站只有十分鐘路程，附近有學校，敎堂和公園，我常常到公園散步。

從我家走約七分鐘，便是繁盛的大街。那裡有一座戲院、中國餐館、西餐館，還有超級市場、洗衣店和幾間服裝店。購物中心裡面有超級市場、洗衣店和幾間服裝店。購物中心旁是社區中心。逢星期六，我都到那裡上中文課，放學後便和媽媽去購物中心購物。我有時也會到社區中心對面的圖書館借一些書回家看。我很喜歡我家附近的環境，交通又方便，設施很完善，街道也很清

一

家在倫敦

Figure 4.5 Page from a book produced in Britain by Chinese teachers who teach in Chinese community schools for use in such schools in Britain. It uses pictures and text that relate to the environment of the children reading the book.

bypass many of the criticisms aimed at imported materials because they have been developed to meet the needs of children overseas. In many cases, they are produced to local norms and therefore do not stand out from the books which children use in mainstream schools (Figure 4.5).

Does quality count?

At the beginning of our research, we were aware that many teachers had serious reservations about quality differences in paper, printing and illustrations, arguing that important status messages are communicated to children when books in other languages do not match the standards of other classroom materials. Keiner (1991), for instance, raises this as an issue in Jewish schools where children are confronted with an exciting array of commercially produced books in English, alongside Hebrew books which fail to speak to their experience or create the same visual impact. Teachers at Thomas Buxton Junior School expressed similar views:

> I've noticed that children don't take the Bengali ones – the ones that are less good in quality, the cheaper ones – by choice. They seem to treat them as being slightly inferior. I presume it is something to do with the feel of the book, the quality of it.

One of the questions we wanted to address was whether teachers' concerns were justified. Do children notice a difference in production standards and, if so, do they express any preferences? And do teachers working in community schools share the worries of their mainstream colleagues? Perceptions of what is aesthetically pleasing vary from one group to another. Is it possible that there is a cultural component in our choices? The same books felt to be inferior by monolingual teachers whose expectations have been moulded by western publishing may be evaluated more favourably by bilingual teachers who have a broader range of experience.

During our visits to schools, both monolingual and bilingual teachers often expressed a need for more books in other languages produced to a standard equivalent to other materials in the classroom. It is not clear whether this is because there is genuine agreement as to what constitutes high standards of production. As one teacher commented, 'We need more glossy hardbacks with bright rather than bland colours and good paper rather than toilet paper.' Teachers spoke, too, of imported books as being 'thin and flimsy' and print and pictures 'not being very good'. However, they also expressed concerns at the cost of 'expensively produced' British books. With continued cutbacks and lack of funds in schools, they say they feel torn between the resources they would like to see in the classroom and the ones they can afford. They make do with books which have been in the school for years. This is particularly true in community schools where there is often no money at all to buy new resources.

To what extent, however, do children's opinions reflect those of their teachers? Part of the Project fieldwork was a case study where children were shown two books: one produced in India and the other in Canada. This study (see overleaf) showed two things: first, that children were aware of and could describe differences in style of illustration, and quality of printing and paper; and secondly, that the Indian-produced book was well-liked by many children and certainly not thought to be inferior. Overall, the children's comments suggested that they noticed quality differences in imported books.

Sometimes their comments were neutral, simply indicating that they were aware of the difference: 'A book from India is just a different style completely. I can tell which one's from here [the UK].' On other occasions, they indicated that they shared the views of many teachers: 'You expect a higher quality to come from England or America or something because it's western.'

Nevertheless, many of the children we talked to said they liked the feel of books produced abroad. One child pointed out, 'I prefer the ones produced in India. I don't know why, I just prefer the Indian ones.' This seems to contradict the concerns of teachers. Children's comments suggest that, despite quality differences, there is certainly a place for imported books in the classroom – the difference between these and other books being, in many ways, a positive feature.

Case study: Does quality count?

As part of the Project fieldwork we showed children two picture dictionaries (Figures 4.6 and 4.7). Both are available in the UK and, although similar in content and format, one was produced in India, the other in Canada. The India-produced book was printed on thick cartridge-like paper with muted colours and realistic illustrations; the one produced in Canada was printed on glossy paper in bright colours, with cartoon-style pictures. We asked the children to describe the paper used, the quality of printing and the style of illustrations. The terms they used are given in Table 4.1 below. While these terms are not the same as those used by professionals they demonstrate that children are very receptive to such issues. A comment from a bilingual child at the Brent Indian Association Gujarati school illustrates this: 'The Gujarati books we buy from England, they're all glossed. And the ones from India, they have no gloss.'

Table 4.1 **Words children used to describe paper, quality of printing and style of illustration in two dictionaries.**

	Dictionary produced in India	**Dictionary produced in Canada**
Paper	rough	smooth
	hard	soft
	recycled	glossy
	sugar paper	sticky
	plain paper	shiny
		plastic
		slippery
Quality of printing	dull	bright
	dark	light
		colourful
Style of illustrations	adultish	babyish
	realistic	cartoonish
	scribbly	funny
		comical

Figure 4.6 Front cover and page from *Star children's picture dictionary* compiled by Babita Verma. New Delhi: Star Publications PVT Ltd, 1992

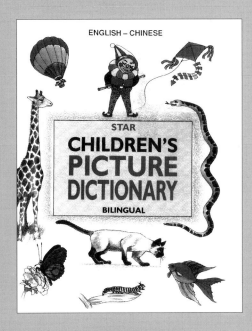

Figure 4.7 Front cover and page from *Cantonese heritage dictionary*. Toronto: Editions Réynyi Inc, 1989

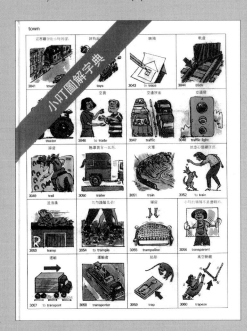

Dual language books

Books in other languages can be an important part of children's experience of other scripts and languages. The single language editions discussed in the previous section are of particular interest to two main groups: recently arrived children already literate in their first language(s) and children born in the new country who have learned to read their community language. Dual language books are accessible to a wider range of readers, including monolingual children.

The first dual language books in the UK date back to the early 1980s. It is easy to understand their appeal. Many monolingual teachers felt insecure about giving children books in languages and scripts which they didn't understand: without a detailed knowledge of other languages and cultures, they were often unconfident about talking to children about what they were reading. Dual language books thus offered a welcome alternative, the English text allowing equal access to monolingual and bilingual readers.

Folk tales and myths

Figure 4.8 Double page spread from *The tiger and the woodpecker* by Aruna Ajitsaria, illustrated by Judy Cobden, Panjabi translation by Surinder Attariwala. London: Middlesex Polytechnic, Reading Materials for Minority Groups Project, 1984

The early dual language books were folk tales and myths, selected for their universal appeal.

Fiction for older children

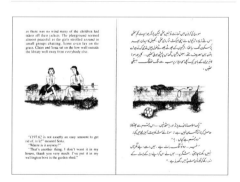

Figure 4.11 Double page spread from *Woman with the pushchair* by Steve Kaufman, illustrated by Kamal Surti, Urdu translation: Qamar Zamani, London: Mantra Publishing Ltd, 1993

Most dual texts are produced for younger children. However, Mantra is one publisher which caters for children in the eight to thirteen age range with their 'One to one' series.

Adaptations of existing English books

Figure 4.9 Page from *Princess Smartypants* by Babette Cole, Urdu translation by Rehana Ahmad. Hayes: Magi Publications, 1992

Many dual texts are adaptations of existing English books. In most cases these are good quality picture books selected because they have ample space for the addition of a second language.

School-produced books

Figure 4.12 Dual text produced by children at Cranford Infant School

Some teachers work with children and parents to 'publish' dual texts for use within the school. The stories often originate from children's writing and they are handwritten or word-processed in both languages with pasted-in drawings.

Books produced by local education authorities

Figure 4.10 Page from *The stupid crocodile* by Felicity Hidderley, Bengali translation: Benu Roy. Isleworth: Primary Community Language Service, Hounslow, nd

Locally produced resources are often very effective because they are designed with a specific user-group in mind. Most resources of this kind are produced within a limited budget: they usually have black and white line illustrations, word-processed or handwritten text and are printed on cheap paper.

Information books

Figure 4.13 Page from *Frogs* edited by Jennie Ingham, Gujarati translation by Niru Desai. London: Macdonald & Co (Publishers) Ltd, 1987

There are very few dual text information books. *Frogs* is one of a range of titles available in English and Bengali, Gujarati, Panjabi and Urdu.

Perceptions of dual language books

Teachers' views on dual language books

It is some years since dual language books were introduced in UK schools, though many of us recall their enthusiastic reception. Their more recent arrival in Canadian schools has met with equally favourable reactions. Feuerverger (1994) describes the excitement of children and teachers in Crescent Town School in Toronto at the introduction of bilingual books, drawing attention to their potential for adding 'a wider perspective to what it means to be Canadian.' Sheila Byram, an ESL teacher at the school, talks about the ways in which books in other languages, and particularly dual language texts, can promote pride in cultural identity:

> [Bilingual children] can sit together with a few children and have them read the first language, and others read the English and they can kind of understand what the English means because they read the Chinese, for example ... [Children] see the world from a different perspective. They are intrigued by the different sounds. I think there's a value in that. To know that there are many different languages in the world and to realize that ours is just one. It's a humbling experience. (Feuerverger, 1994, p. 135)

She describes this view of dual texts as widespread in the school. On one occasion,

when a Chinese child had finished reading, an Iranian boy was heard to say he wished that he could read Chinese. The researcher who witnessed this exchange commented:

> As a result, students learn to admire and respect those who come from other backgrounds and languages, rather than to be prejudiced against them. I believe that this is such an important part of multicultural teaching. (Feuerverger, 1994, p. 136)

The situation in British schools is, of course, a little different. In Canada, 'new Canadians' are still arriving in large numbers. In Britain, although many children are still coming, either to join their families or as refugees from countries like Bosnia and Somalia, the vast majority have been born in Britain. The main aim of dual language books for these children is not to act as a bridge to literacy in English, but to offer opportunities for developing literacy skills in their community or heritage language.

Teachers in the Project schools identified various uses for dual language books. Like their Canadian colleagues, they saw the potential for raising all children's awareness of multiculturalism through exposure to different languages and scripts. They also saw dual language books as a valuable bridge between home and school, making it possible, for instance, for parents, grandparents and others literate in the community language to read with their children. This view was confirmed by the children we talked to. Eleven-year-old Asma described how her mother reads the Urdu first and then she repeats it. Seven-year-old Shamima said she enjoyed listening to her big sister read the Bengali text.

However, dual language books have proved a good deal more controversial than single language resources. Teachers in community schools, in particular, are sometimes adamant that they are unhelpful in community language teaching. As a teacher in the Ramgarhia

Sabha Sunday School pointed out, children who are learning to read and write Panjabi tend to be 'lazy … It's so easy for them to just concentrate on the English.' Many teachers in the other community schools made similar comments. However, some had a rather more sanguine view, acknowledging that dual language books can in fact act as a bridge to literacy for children whose dominant language is now English. A teacher in the Hounslow Chinese school pointed out that the dual texts in their library were more popular than the books in Chinese only: 'I think the pupils can relate to them more.' Other teachers recognized the value of dual texts in extending the range of reading material available for children.

However, the reservations about dual language books are not limited to community schools. Teachers in mainstream schools expressed similar concerns:

> Personally, I don't like two languages in one book because each should have its own status … You get into the mode of one language. I wouldn't want to read a book in two languages.

Children's views on dual language books

As part of the Project we also asked children what they thought about dual language books. All children – monolingual and bilingual – showed an awareness of the potential benefits of these books. Eleven-year-old Mira, for instance, pointed out that:

> You can work with an adult and learn how to read Gujarati at the same time as reading it in English … Those who don't know English can read the Gujarati and those who don't know Gujarati can read the English.

There is every reason to suppose that monolingual English-speaking children benefit greatly from exposure to books in other languages and are aware of their usefulness. Six-year-old Brandon pointed out that:

> In case somebody in this language came to our class and they didn't know English, they could read that [pointing to the other language]. Then when they came to know English, they could read English.

Eight-year-old Jonathan was clearly thinking along similar lines: 'Sometimes somebody might come to your house and want to read some books and they can't speak English.' He also saw the possibilities for collaborative work: 'Two different people might want to read it.'

While monolingual children clearly benefit from reading dual language books alongside bilingual peers, they are also able to develop their awareness while working independently. A group of seven-year-olds at Barham Primary School talked about pretending to read the non-English text 'for fun'. They also offered interesting insights into the kinds of hypotheses they were developing about how different languages work. Some children clearly think that word-order remains the same, irrespective of the language, and that in a translation, the two texts can be matched word for word, with each taking up the same amount of space on the page. 'It's just that sometimes we think it's a wrong word because this bit's shorter or longer.' In comments such as this, there is potential for much valuable discussion among the children themselves and as well as with the teacher.

We also asked about children's preferences: given a free choice, would they take a single language or a dual language book? Some were clear that their decision would be based on subject rather than the language format of the book. Ten-year-old Kiron, for instance, summed this up simply in terms of 'I'd take whichever one I thought was a more interesting story.' Other children confirmed the suspicions of community language teachers. One said he would choose the dual text because he 'knew English better'; another explained that he would take the single language book because 'otherwise I would just read the English and not make the effort to read Bengali.' However, these views were by no means universal. A number of children talked of the support that dual texts can offer when they are reading the community language – 'because you get the idea of what they're saying', or because 'you can learn quicker than if there's just one language.'

A complex picture emerges from this discussion of dual language books. They have the potential to act as a bridge between the languages of school and home; they also have the effect of raising monolingual children's awareness of, and interest in, other languages. However, views around their usefulness in promoting literacy in community languages are more divided. Some teachers and children feel that the presence of English removes the motivation for persevering with the community language. In contrast, other teachers – and children – point to the security blanket which dual language books can offer.

These conflicting views point to the need to think very carefully about how best to use dual language books. Different solutions will be better suited to different situations. The underlying principle must be to match the approach to the needs of the particular children. Our own research suggests that even very young children can be extremely articulate about what precisely these needs may be.

Design issues in dual language books

The design of bilingual children's books raises some interesting issues for typographers ranging from choice of typefaces to the graphic organization of two languages on a page. Dual texts for children pose additional questions because they contain pictures: where should the texts be placed in relation to the pictures?

Designers, like teachers, are particularly interested in how people read. They can offer valuable insights on the ways in which the layout, typography and production features hinder or enhance the reader's interaction with the text.

Dual texts: books, chapters or pages?

Dual texts can be organized in a number of different ways: as whole books, as sections or chapters, as double-page spreads or as single pages.

Some of the most innovative approaches to designing dual texts occur at the level of the book as a whole. Such approaches play with our conventional notions of what a book is and with our strategies for reading. An example of a dual text that falls into this category is Brian Wildsmith's *The tunnel/Le tunnel* (OUP, 1993). This book is a dual text in French and English. The cover at one end of the book is in French and, opening the book from this end, the French text is dominant (it is placed above the English text and is in bold type); when readers get to the middle of the book, they are invited to turn the book around and read from the other cover which has the title in English and opens onto pages where the English text takes the dominant role (see

Figure 4.14 Two pages from *The tunnel/Le tunnel* by Brian Wildsmith, French translation by Anne-Marie Dalmais. Oxford: Oxford University Press, 1993

In this dual text in French and English, the French text is predominant in one half of the book, the English in the other. The dominant language is placed above the other and set in bold type.

Un beau jour, une petite taupe française, appelée Pierre, reçut une lettre de son cousin Marcus qui vivait en Angleterre, disant qu'il aimerait venir en France.

One day a little French mole called Pierre got a letter from his cousin Marcus who lived in England, saying he would like to come to France.

One day a little English mole called Marcus wrote a letter to his cousin Pierre who lived in France.

Un beau jour, une petite taupe anglaise, appelée Marcus, écrivit une lettre à son cousin Pierre, qui vivait en France.

Figure 4.14). Another dual text that falls into this category is *The moving mango tree* (Partnership Publishing, 1992) where equal status is given to two languages that run in different directions by making one book out of two, one opening left to right and the other right to left. The illustrations are not repeated, rather they relate across both texts, and appear sometimes in the English and sometimes in the Urdu (see Figure 4.15).

Very occasionally dual texts function at the level of the section or the chapter. *Découvrez ... who stole Granny?* (Gemini Books, 1990), for instance, is a bilingual 'choose your own adventure' story about a French-speaking brother and sister who are visiting their grandmother in English-speaking Ontario. The first chapter appears in two languages, the English occupying the left-hand page and the French the right-hand page. At the end of this first chapter, the reader is invited to choose between two possible routes:

Figure 4.15 A spread from *The moving mango tree and other tales* by Zohra Jabeen, illustrated by Georgia Woollard. Bradford: Partnership Publishing, 1992

In this dual text, the English opens left to right, and the Urdu right to left. Readers view a 'quadruple spread' and the illustrations appear sometimes in the English section and sometimes in the Urdu.

Figure 4.16 Double page spread from *Découvrez ... who stole Granny?* by Viv Edwards & Nicole Bérubé. Clevedon: Gemini Books Ltd, 1990

A dual text where, after a bilingual introduction, the language of each chapter is in French or English according to the situation.

What should I do? If you think I ought to find out first turn to page 27. If you think I ought to phone immediately for an ambulance, turn to page 15.

After the bilingual introduction, the language of each new chapter is determined by the situation. Phone conversations with the emergency operator and the police, for instance, take place in English. Conversations between the Francophone hero and heroine of the adventure take place in French. To make your way through the book, you have to use both languages (see Figure 4.16).

Most dual texts, however, are organized at the level of the double page spread, or the single page. Some page designs are based on a grid which means that the text and pictures fall in the same position on each page or double spread throughout the book (see Figure 4.17). In some books, the placing of illustration and text varies from page to page and the text is fitted within or around the illustrations (see Figure 4.18).

Words and pictures on a page

Within the constraints of the page or double page spread there are many ways of organizing text and pictures. Goldsmith (1984) summarizes research that looks at the use of pictures in educational material. Of the work she reviews, Smith & Watkins (1972) and Brandt (1945) consider the relationship between text and pictures on a page or series of pages.

Smith & Watkins identify factors that need to be taken into account in designing books with text and pictures for children: age and ability of child, reading strategy, reading time allowed, type of material, comprehensibility of pictures and, indeed, their necessity. Their work suggests there can be no one solution to text/picture relationships and that a range of approaches may suit a range of purposes.

He caught a young eagle and brought it home. He put it among his hens and ducks and turkeys, and gave it chicken food to eat, even though it was an eagle, the king of birds.

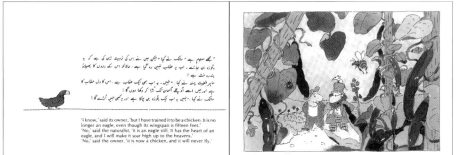

'I know,' said its owner, 'but I have trained it to be a chicken. It is no longer an eagle, even though its wingspan is fifteen feet.'
'No,' said the naturalist, 'it is an eagle still. It has the heart of an eagle, and I will make it soar high up to the heavens.'
'No,' said the owner, 'it is now a chicken, and it will never fly.'

Figure 4.17 Two double page spreads from *The eagle that would not fly* by James Aggrey, illustrated by Wolf Erlbruch, Urdu translation by Rehana Ahmad. Hayes: Magi Publications, 1988

This is an example of a dual language book where texts and pictures are placed in the same relative position on each double page spread.

Abba put his head round the door.

Kevin's Mum had noticed something too.
"Tahir!" she shouted. "Where is my yellow chair?"
Tahir was surprised. "I don't know. Honest."

Figure 4.18 Two pages from *The magic ink* by Anna Robinson, illustrated by Wendy Lewis, Panjabi translation by S. S. Kang. London: Mantra Publishing Limited, 1986

In this design the position of the texts varies from page to page.

Brandt's work was about eye movements and he reported that if text and pictures are placed horizontally, the text receives more attention if the picture is on the left. He proposes that this is because the picture has more attraction value than the text and that reading conventions make it natural to move to the right. These observations suggest that when direction of reading is right–left (not left–right as Brandt's test material), putting the picture on the right may benefit the reader.

Dual texts, however, present another dimension to the relationship between words and pictures. It is not just a picture/text relationship, but picture/text/text configuration that has to be considered. This results in many options for organization. Take first that of two texts: within a page or double page spread the most common arrangement is for one text to be placed above the other in any one of the configurations shown in Table 4.2. Of these three arrangements, the most widely used is placing one text above the other, the texts separated by space. When illustrations are added, however, the options for page layout increase as shown in Table 4.3 on the next page.

Table 4.2 **Configurations for setting dual texts with one text above the other**

How the text is arranged	**Visual configuration**
a directly above the other separated by space	xxxx xxx xxx xxx xx xx xxx xxx x x xxxx xxxx oooo ooo ooo ooo oo oo ooo ooo o o oooo ooo
b directly above the other separated by a line or pattern	xxxx xxx xxx xxx xx xx xxx xxx x x xxxx xxxx · oooo ooo ooo ooo oo oo ooo ooo o o oooo ooo

c above the other but staggered right or left	xxxx xxx xxx xxx xx xx xxx
	xxx x x xxxx xxxx
	     oooo ooo ooo ooo oo oo ooo
	     ooo o o oooo ooo

Table 4.3 **Ways of organizing text and pictures in dual texts**

	picture above both texts	picture below both texts	picture between both texts	picture on one page, both texts on the other	picture covering whole page or spread (texts within picture)
one text above other (separated by space)	**1**	**2**	**3**	**4**	**5**

Figure 4.19 Page from *A wet dinner time*, Urdu translation by Qamar Zamani. London: Cambridge University Press and Jennie Ingham Associates Ltd, 1989

And when they had all gone
Mrs Handa had a little dance too.
All on her own.

16

The other two configurations – texts side-by-side and one text vertical, the other horizontal – are used in situations where languages are read in different directions. Of the Project languages Urdu and Chinese raise issues of directionality.

A widely used convention in English/Urdu dual texts is placing the languages side-by-side with English on the left and Urdu on the right – in this way the beginnings of the lines of both languages are at the page edge (Figure 4.19). The nature of the Chinese writing system means that it can be written horizontally or vertically, and many English/Chinese dual texts, therefore, show Chinese running left to right in rows because it is easier to combine with English in this form. There are examples, however, of traditional orientation where the Chinese runs vertically as in Figure 4.20.

When they got to "three" the Tiger jumped up, sweeping the Frog high up into the air with him. The Frog leapt with all his might and jumped even higher. The Tiger had lost the first round.

"That test doesn't count. Let's go onto the river-jump contest," said the Tiger. So they walked over to the river bank. With a shout of "one, two, three" the contest began. But on the count of "one" the Frog once again hopped onto the Tiger's tail. As the Tiger jumped forward, he swept the Frog up with him, tossing him far ahead. Again the Frog had used all his strength to fling himself forward and he beat the Tiger by a long distance.

Figure 4.20 Page from *The tiger and the frog* edited by Hong Chung, illustrated by Jiang Chengan. Hong Kong: Hai Feng Publishing Company, 1983

Using dual texts

The effectiveness of a particular page design depends on how the book is used. In schools we visited, we observed dual texts in various different situations, the most common being storytime with a mixed group of bilingual and monolingual children and either two teachers (one bilingual, one monolingual), or a bilingual teacher. Sometimes the whole story was read (or paraphrased) first in one language, and then in the other; sometimes the languages were alternated one page at a time; and at other times the less familiar language was read using the more familiar language as reference.

Our own observations coincide with those of Martin-Jones *et al.* (1992). When monolingual and bilingual teachers work together, the monolingual teacher retains control. However, when bilingual teachers or assistants assume sole responsibility, they have more scope for using the children's home language throughout and to respond to children's contributions.

But dual language books were also used in other ways: by groups of bilingual children working alone; by groups of monolingual children working alone; and by individual bilingual and monolingual children with or without the help of a bilingual teacher or assistant. We also heard about their use at home with parents and older relations and friends literate in one or both of the languages.

Some page layouts work better in some situations than in others. As part of our fieldwork, we asked teachers for their comments about five alternative arrangements of text and pictures and what they preferred to use in the classroom. Three of the arrangements were chosen because they were widely used and two because the research group considered them innovative.

Sameep and the parrots (Figure 4.21)

Placing a picture between the two texts supports reading the two languages separately: the pictures make a strong divide between the two languages. However, many of the teachers we spoke to felt that this layout encouraged children to focus on one language only, rather than reading the two languages together. One teacher at Ramgarhia Sabha Sunday School, for example, was concerned that: 'With this, the child could quickly concentrate on the English and skip the other language.' A teacher at the Hounslow Chinese School had similar views: 'Most people I know ... would read just the English and forget the other.'

Interestingly, teachers in the mainstream Project schools seemed less bothered about the separation because it allowed them to focus on the differences between languages. A bilingual teacher at Cranford Infant School described one of her teaching strategies thus:

> Sometimes, if they're familiar with another language, I cover it up and go through the English, then I say 'OK now we're going to look at another writing' [and cover up the English].

This way of using dual texts is made easier when the languages are clearly separated.

School dinners (Figure 4.22)

This kind of layout where the picture takes up one page of a double page spread supports reading strategies where both languages are read together. It also allows teachers to use the picture independently of the text, a useful strategy with inexperienced readers. A bilingual teacher at Cranford Infant School, for instance, made the point that

> If the texts are on one page and the picture on the other, you can cover the text and talk about the picture – with the younger ones I prefer something like that.

The snake was very large. It had beautiful red and blue spots on it. But it was very dangerous. Sameep was frightened. He decided he would always wear sandals when he travelled through the forest. He knew that there were lots of snakes crawling in and out of the trees. But perhaps they were frightened of him.

Figure 4.21 A page from *Sameep and the parrots* by Elaine Abrahams, illustrated by Eliana, Urdu version: Zareena Hashmi. Stanmore: Harmony Publishing Ltd, 1986

One text above the other, separated by a picture.

What's for dinner today?

Sausages and chips.

Figure 4.22 A page from *School dinners* by Peter Heaslip, photographs by John Bennett, Panjabi translation by Jaskanwal Kalra. London: Methuen Educational, 1978

Picture on the left, both texts on the right-hand page.

Figure 4.23 Double page spread from *The magic ink* by Anna Robinson, illustrated by Wendy Lewis, Panjabi translation by S. S. Kang. London: Mantra Publishing Limited, 1986

Text within pictures.

Figure 4.24 Double-page spread from *The eagle that would not fly* by James Aggrey, illustrated by Wolf Erlbruch, Urdu translation by Rehana Ahmad. Hayes: Magi Publications, 1988

One text above the other separated by a line, picture on the right.

Figure 4.25 Spread from *The moving mango tree and other tales* by Zohra Jabeen, illustrated by Georgia Woollard. Bradford: Partnership Publishing, 1992

Texts side-by-side, picture above both texts. Note the way the picture has been reversed.

The magic ink (Figure 4.23)

In this example the picture covers the whole page and the texts are placed one above the other. Some teachers thought it better to keep text and pictures separate. As one commented, 'As far as design is concerned, you could have laid that [text] somewhere else so the picture is complete'. This kind of layout means that the position of the texts is likely to change from page to page because it has to be fitted in where there is space within the illustration.

The eagle that would not fly (Figure 4.24)

We did not find many dual texts that used a line to separate the two languages from each other and this was a solution that was new to most of the teachers we interviewed. However, many liked this layout. They thought it would allow the texts to be read together and compared but, at the same time, the graphic separation would make it easier to read one language independently without being distracted by the other.

The moving mango tree (Figure 4.25)

The moving mango tree is an innovative approach to the problem of combining languages which run from right to left and left to right. It is also the only example we discovered. None of the teachers we spoke to had used this book with children. Many, however, saw this arrangement as a very successful way of dealing with the problem of language directionality, though some also thought it might be cumbersome. However, the large format makes it ideal for use in small groups of older children reading independently of the teacher, or in groups of younger children, working with a bilingual adult.

The arrangement of words and pictures in dual texts is a complex issue: not only are there many ways of doing it, but there is clearly a link between some page layouts and how these books can be most effectively used as learning devices.

Status in dual texts

Dual texts are frequently criticized because the two languages are not given equal status (Kumar, 1988; Chatterji, 1991). A number of factors are perceived by teachers and children as making one language appear more important than the other. The questions and observations presented in Table 4.4 below draw attention to some of these issues.

Table 4.4 **Status issues in dual texts**

	Issues	**Key questions**
Typography	One script takes precedence over the other in a dual text	*Are typographic features such as size, space, weight and colour applied consistently across both languages?*
	One script is of a higher quality than the other in a dual text	*What messages are sent to readers when the English text is typeset, and the other is handwritten?*
Production	The typography/page layout has been compromised because of the printing process	*Has the other language been squashed in to fit an existing single language page?*
Language	The translation of the non-English text in a dual text is inappropriate	*Is the translation suitable for educational use?*
	The text is inaccessible to the audience	*Is the language too formal or literary?*

Figure 4.26 *The elves and the shoemaker and other tales.* Ilford: Newham Women's Community Writing Group, 1983 (English and Urdu)

Figure 4.27 *The elves and the shoemaker and other tales.* Ilford: Newham Women's Community Writing Group, 1983 (English and Panjabi)

Figure 4.28 *The elves and the shoemaker and other tales.* Ilford: Newham Women's Community Writing Group, 1983 (English and Gujarati)

Figures 4.26 – 4.28 **The first set of spreads used in the fieldwork. The texts are typed or handwritten; the pictures are black and white.**

Typography

Dual texts present a different set of typographic problems to those in single language books: this is partly because there are two texts rather than one, and partly, in the case of the Project languages, because both Latin and non-Latin alphabets are used. The typographic treatment of the two languages and the way they are placed in relation to each other, and on the page, are likely to have implications for whether or not these languages are seen to be equally important by readers.

Factors that affect typographic status include mode (whether text has been typeset, word processed or handwritten), use of space, size, and amount of text. In an ideal dual text the way in which these factors have been handled helps to make sure that one language is not seen as more important than the other.

Project fieldwork included discussions about typographic issues with monolingual and bilingual children in each of the schools we visited. Groups of children in different age groups were shown two sets of dual texts which raised a number of status issues. The first consisted of three versions of *The elves and the shoemaker and other tales* (1983): English/Gujarati, English/Panjabi and English/Urdu. The pictures are in black and white, the English text is set on a typewriter and the non-Latin script is handwritten (Figures 4.26–4.28). In the second set: *Anita and the magician* (1987), *The enchanted palace* (1985) and *The hare and the tortoise* (1985), both texts are typeset and the pictures are in colour (Figures 4.29–4.31). The children's comments left little doubt about their awareness of and definite views on issues of typographic status.

Mode of writing

One of the most important typographic status issues in dual texts centres around

"Little boy, check what's in my other hand," said Paul. "Nothing," said Paul. The children watched Fantismo closely. He flipped the coin with his left hand and caught it in his right. Opening his palms, each one contained a pound.

''ਕਾਕਾ, ਤੂੰ ਦੇਖ ਮੇਰੇ ਦੂਜੇ ਹੱਥ ਵਿਚ ਕੀ ਹੈ?'' ''ਕੁਝ ਵੀ ਨਹੀਂ,'' ਪਾਲ ਨੇ ਉੱਤਰ ਦਿਤਾ। ਤੇ ਦੇਰ ਘੰਚੇ ਫੈਂਟਿਸ਼ੋ ਨੂੰ ਧਿਆਨ ਨਾਲ ਵੇਖਦਾ ਰਹਿਆ। ਉਹਨੇ ਸਿੱਕੇ ਨੂੰ ਆਪਟੇ ਖੱਬੇ ਹੱਥ ਨਾਲ ਉਡਾਇਆ ਤੇ ਸੱਜੇ ਹੱਥ ਵਿਚ ਵੜ ਲਿਆ। ਫਿਰ ਉਹਨੇ ਆਪਟਿਆਂ ਮੁਠੀਆਂ ਖਲੋਇਆਂ ਤੇ ਦੋਹਾਂ ਵਿਚ ਇਕ ਇਕ ਪਾਉਂਡ ਦਾ ਸਿੱਕਾ ਸੀ।

Figure 4.29 Double page spread from *Anita and the magician* by Swaran Chandan, illustrated by Keir Wickenham, edited by Gail Chester. Hayes: Magi Publications, 1987

Figure 4.30 Double page spread from *The enchanted palace* by Ashim Bhattacharya & Champaka Basu, illustrated by Amanda Welch, edited by Jennie Ingham. London: Luzac & Co. Ltd, 1985

The Prince was so entranced that years went by as he gazed at her without even a blink. Until, one day, he noticed, on her pillow, a golden stick. Moving forward quietly, he picked it up. No sooner had he done so than he saw, on the other side of the pillow, a silver stick. He held both the sticks in his hands, idly playing with them, and wondering where they had come from. And, while he did so, the gold stick fell on the Princess's cheek.

All at once the blanket of lotus blossoms shivered, the golden bed gently shook, and the Princess rubbed her eyes, stretched and woke up. As her hands and legs appeared, all the golden petals fell.

She gazed in wonder at the Prince for he had saved her.

And then she told him this strange story.

Figure 4.31 Double page spread from *The hare and the tortoise* by Gabriel Douloubakas, illustrated by Mikel Horl, edited by Jennie Ingham. London: Luzac & Co. Ltd, 1985

The Hare went up to to the Tortoise thinking to himself, "What have I got to fear from a tortoise?" and he said "What a nice day, my lovely friend". The Tortoise answered, "Yes, my dear Hare, a very nice and peaceful day, not even a movement of a leaf".

The Hare jumped about happily and suddenly he said to the Tortoise, "I have a good idea".

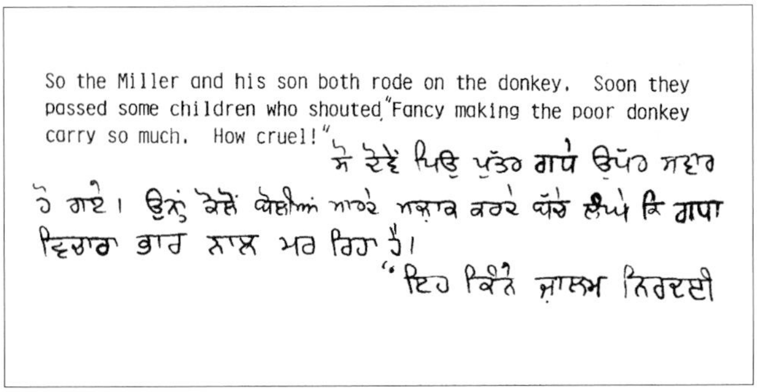

Figure 4.32 Detail from *The elves and the shoemaker and other tales*, English and Panjabi edition. Ilford: Newham Women's Community Writing Group, 1983

Different modes of text presentation, in this case typing and handwriting, can make one language appear more important than the other.

different modes of presentation being used for each of the languages. If one language is handwritten and the other typeset, for example, the typeset language can often seem better quality and therefore more important. Many dual texts have the English typeset while the other language script is produced in a lower resolution form, such as word processing or handwriting. We explored the extent to which children noticed such status differences by showing double page spreads from each of the two sets. We asked: 'Tell me what you think about the two languages in each book, and the way the writing's been done'. The resulting discussions suggest that children were both aware of and concerned about the use of different modes and the status implications this has.

Nine-year-old Noman at Havelock Primary, for example, looking at the text in versions of *The elves and the shoemaker*, thought: 'Better to make them the same. If you're going to make one wibbly wobbly, you might as well make all of them.' A bilingual eleven-year-old at Ahmadiyya Muslim Women's Association had similar views, pointing out that if both languages in *The elves and the shoemaker* had been typed, they would at least be the same (Figure 4.32).

Teachers, also, were concerned about such differences and had noticed that they affected the ways in which children used dual texts.

> They'll [children] read the nicely printed professional-looking [typeset] English text … they might look at the other rather subsidiary [handwritten] text . But if they have any problems at all they certainly won't consider it …. There is a place for handwritten texts but, in a dual text, both languages should be the same.

As well as noticing differences in the way the texts were written, some children also had views about whether handwriting or typesetting was more effective. Some, for example,

Figure 4.33 Detail
from *The elves and
the shoemaker and
other tales*, English
and Gujarati edition.
Ilford: Newham
Women's
Community Writing
Group, 1983

A Miller and his son were taking their donkey to market. On their
way they passed some girls who shouted,"Fancy walking when they
could be riding. How stupid!"

એક ધંટીવાળો ડોસો અને તેનો દીકરો, તેમના ગધેડાને બજારમાં
લઈ જતા હતા. રસ્તામાં તેમને પોડી છોકરીઓ મળી. છોકરીઓ
કહે, "છતે ગધેડે આ લોકો ચાલીને જાય છે. કેવા મૂર્ખ છે!"

Figure 4.34 Detail
from *The elves and
the shoemaker and
other tales*, English
and Panjabi edition.
Ilford: Newham
Women's
Community Writing
Group, 1983

So the Miller and his son both rode on the donkey. Soon they
passed some children who shouted,"Fancy making the poor donkey
carry so much. How cruel!"
ਸੋ ਰੇਲ੍ਹੇ ਮਿਲ੍ਹ ਪੁੱਤਰ ਉਪਰ ਚੜ੍ਹੇ ਸਵਾਰ
ਤੇ ਗਏ। ਉਨ੍ਹ ਐਸੇ ਬੱਚਿਆਂ ਨਾਲ ਸੜਕ ਕਰਦੇ ਚੱਲੇ ਕੀ ਗਧਾ
ਵਿਚਾਰ ਭਾਰ ਨਾਲ ਮਰ ਗਿਆ ਹੈ।
"ਇਹ ਕਿੰਨੇ ਜ਼ਾਲਮ ਨਿਰਦਈ

Figures 4.33 and 4.34 show inconsistency in line spacing
from language to language.

Figure 4.35 Detail
from *Anita and the
magician* by Swaran
Chandan. Hayes:
Magi Publications,
1987

"Little boy, check what's in my other hand."
"Nothing," said Paul. The children watched
Fantismo closely. He flipped the coin with his
left hand and caught it in his right. Opening his
palms, each one contained a pound.

"ਝਾਬਾ, ਤੂੰ ਦੱਸ ਮੇਰੇ ਦੂਜੇ ਹੱਥ ਵਿਚ ਕੀ ਹੈ?"
"ਕੁਝ ਵੀ ਨਹੀਂ," ਪਾਲ ਨੇ ਉਤੱਰ ਦਿੱਤਾ ਤੇ ਫੇਰ ਬੱਚੇ
ਫੈਂਟਿਸਮੇ ਨੂੰ ਧਿਆਨ ਨਾਲ ਵੇਖਣ ਲੱਗੇ। ਉਸਨੇ ਸਿੱਕੇ ਨੂੰ
ਆਪਣੇ ਖੱਬੇ ਹੱਥ ਨਾਲ ਉਛਾਲਿਆ ਤੇ ਸੱਜੇ ਹੱਥ ਵਿਚ ਝੱਟ
ਲਿਆ। ਫੇਰ ਉਸਨੇ ਆਪਣੀਆਂ ਮੁਠੀਆਂ ਖੋਲ੍ਹੀਆਂ ਤੇ ਦੋਹਾਂ
ਵਿਚ ਇੱਕ ਇੱਕ ਪਾਉਂਡ ਦਾ ਸਿੱਕਾ ਸੀ।

Figure 4.36 Detail
from *The enchanted
palace* by Ashim
Bhattacharya &
Champaka Basu,
edited by Jennie
Ingham. London:
Luzac & Co. Ltd,
1985

Many, many years ago, there was a terrible demon, who wanted the Princess for
himself. He captured her and, when she refused to marry him, he put a curse on her.
The demon's grandmother, who was a witch, was left to guard her and the
Princess became the witch's slave. Everytime she wished to be attended to, the witch
used to wake up the Princess with a golden stick. Gradually, she grew fond of
the Princess. The witch told her that the only way the curse could be removed
was by killing the demon.

অনেক অনেক বছর আগে একটি ভয়ংকর রাক্ষস ছিল যে রাজকুমারীকে বিয়ে করতে চাইত।
রাক্ষসটি তাকে ধরে আনল এবং যখন রাজকুমারী তাকে বিয়ে করতে চাইল না সে তাকে অভিশাপ
দিল। রাক্ষসটি তার ডাইনী ঠাকুমাকে রাজকুমারীর পাহারায় নিযুক্ত করল এবং রাজকুমারী
ডাইনীটির দাসীতে পরিণত হল। যখনই রাজকুমারী ডাইনীটিকে প্রয়োজন হত সে সোনার কাঠিটির সাহায্যে
রাজকুমারীর ঘুম ভাঙাত। ধীরে ধীরে সে রাজকুমারীকে পছন্দ করতে আরম্ভ করল। ডাইনীটি
তাকে বলল শুধুমাত্র রাক্ষসটিকে হত্যা করলেই তার ওপর থেকে অভিশাপ বিলুপ্ত হবে।

Figures 4.35 and 4.36 show consistent treatment of line
spacing. However, Figure 4.35 was praised by children,
but the line spacing in Figure 4.36 was thought to be too
close. Interestingly, the next edition of this book, published by Jennie Ingham Associates, has shorter lines of
type adequately spaced.

preferred handwriting, as shown in the following remarks from a group of ten- and
eleven-year-olds at the Brent Indian
Association Gujarati School:

> Both texts should be handwritten so
> people can learn to write the letters.

> It makes it easier to read when it's done by
> hand because you're used to those shapes.

Some children, however, complained that
handwritten text was more difficult to read.
Consistency in presentation therefore seems
to be a key issue: the mode of presentation
should be the same for both texts in a dual
text. It is possible, for instance, that two handwritten texts might be a more acceptable solution in terms of status than a typeset English
version and a handwritten non-Latin. Indeed,
for a script with a strong calligraphic tradition
such as Urdu, handwriting is entirely appropriate and could be supported by a well-
handwritten English text.

Use of space

Space is a key issue in typography. Careful use
of space affects both legibility, and the way in
which readers navigate a page of text. In the
dual texts we looked at, the spacing between
lines and words was often different for the two
languages. Again, this can have the effect of
making one language appear more significant
than the other.

While children could not tell us their views
in terms of legibility and navigation, they
clearly noticed differences in spacing in the
books we showed them. In the Gujarati and
Panjabi editions of *The elves and the shoemaker*, there is considerable variation in the line
spacing between the English and the other
language (Figures 4.33 and 4.34). This variation encouraged children to express such
views as, 'The Panjabi is bigger and spaced
out a lot more than the zEnglish is'.

Anita and the magician was consistently
singled out by children as a 'good example'.
They noted that both typefaces looked the

same size, and that it was 'clear and fat', and that the type was set with plenty of space around it (Figure 4.35). *The enchanted palace*, on the other hand, provoked the comment: 'That one looks like it's all squashed in' (Figure 4.36).

Size of letterforms and amount of text

Size of letterforms and amount of text on the page are two characteristics readily noticed by readers. In a dual text, or indeed any piece of bilingual typography, some languages take up more space than others. In many of the dual texts we have seen, changing the size of one of the scripts is a common solution to this problem, but this raises the issue of relative size and importance – 'this one's bigger so it's more important.' In books designed with a grid that accommodates texts of different lengths on a page, text size and spacing can be kept constant. But, when one language takes up more space than the other, some bilingual children were concerned about the balance between the languages. For instance, a nine-year-old at Thomas Buxton Junior said of the pages from the Gujarati edition of *The elves and the shoemaker* illustrated in Figure 4.28

that: 'This has little things to say and that has lots of things to say'.

Small letterforms also tended to be associated with difficulty, provoking comments such as:

> The words are smaller, you can tell they're for older children – the bigger the words, the younger the children.

> This one is bigger, so it's easier to read … the pictures are bigger and the writing's bigger as well.

Production status

The way dual texts are produced can also have status implications. Often, for example, when mainstream publishers produce dual texts, they choose an already popular single language text and bring out a new edition combining English with a variety of other languages. Although these books meet the same production standards as mainstream single language books, they can still present inequalities in the status given to the two languages.

For such books to be cost-effective, the same printing plates have to be used for the

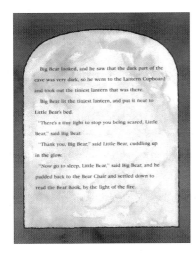 

Figure 4.37 Page from *Can't you sleep, Little Bear?* by Martin Waddell & Barbara Firth. London: Walker Books, 1990

Figure 4.38 Panjabi translation by Jaspal Singh Grewal. Hayes: Magi Publications, 1993

The dual text version uses the same printing plates for the colour illustrations; the English text is reset to accommodate the other language.

Then Haruna had a problem. "There's a tiger in my classroom," she said. "My teacher is sitting on top of the cupboard and he's too frightened to come down."

All the children in the playground knew what to do. They all said immediately...

"Send for Sohail!"

Now whenever Sohail was sent for, he always came, quick as a flash.

"A tiger," he remarked . "That's only a small problem. Didn't you know that tigers love milk?" and he went to the milkman and got thirty bottles of milk.

"Come on tiger," he shouted, as he poured all the milk into a dustbin lid. The tiger looked wary, but very slowly came out and had a big, big drink. Then before the tiger could blink, Sohail slipped a skipping-rope around his neck and took him back to the zoo.

Figure 4.39   An opening from *Send for Sohail!* by Grange Road First School, Bradford, illustrated by Sean Pike. Bradford: Partnership Publishing, 1993

An example of a dual text that successfully addresses the issue of directionality. The book opens from the top: an unconventional approach for both languages.

illustrations in all dual language editions. The other language is either fitted into any available space alongside the English, or the English is reset to make sure there is enough space left for the other language. Such rejigging inevitably leads to compromise. If another language has to be fitted into an available space it can mean that the type is set to 'fit the space' rather than being considered in relation to the size of the English or to the needs of the reader. Sometimes, the existing English text is 're-arranged' to make space for another language, and this can mean that what may have originally been designed for children in terms of spacing and typesize becomes less appropriate (Figure 4.37 and 4.38). The position of text in relation to the illustrations can also be significant because the English text can appear to take precedence if it, rather than the other language, relates to the action in the illustrations.

Producing dual texts which combine languages that run from right to left with those that run left to right presents additional problems. Most dual texts incorporating right–left reading languages are therefore produced with the book conventions of left–right reading languages in mind. Readers of Urdu texts therefore have to open the book from the 'wrong' end. Many publishers are aware of this problem, but recognize that they cannot afford to produce single language Urdu editions. Chatterji (1991, p. 4) summarizes the technical problem and implications:

> To produce just one Urdu edition which reads from right to left alongside others which read from left to right would mean producing a complete new set of plates especially for that edition, because of re-sequencing the order of pages. Therefore instead of a plate showing picture 1 on page 1 (as in all the other language editions) picture 1 would have to be on the back page. As a high cost of the printing is in the making of the plates, this would increase the price of that particular edition to an unpayable level.

Despite such limitations, some arrangements do allow for successful incorporation of right–left reading languages.

Where Urdu/English books are designed as dual texts from the outset, there are several innovative approaches to the problem. *Send for Sohail!*, for example, is an English/Urdu book that is landscape format opening from the top, with full-page illustrations on the top half of the spread and the text (English on the left and Urdu on the right) on the bottom half. The two languages have equal directional status and the illustrations relate equally to both texts (Figure 4.39).

Designing dual texts: some considerations

As with any children's book it is important that dual texts are designed so that the text is easy for children to read. What issues do designers need to consider when producing dual texts for children that use Latin and non-Latin scripts?

Designing any children's book means thinking about the user: the typeface, type-size, line length, line spacing and word spacing all have to be appropriate for children. There has been very little research in this field even in books using only the Latin alphabet. Deciding exactly what is appropriate typographically can only be done by seeing what works with children through trialling and evaluation.

Nevertheless, what we do know about legibility research for adults, combined with the small amount of research with children in this area (see Walker, 1993 and Watts & Nisbet, 1974), suggests the following issues are important:

1 Typeface
There is no single typeface that is 'best' for children's books although there are some that are more appropriate than others. In the case

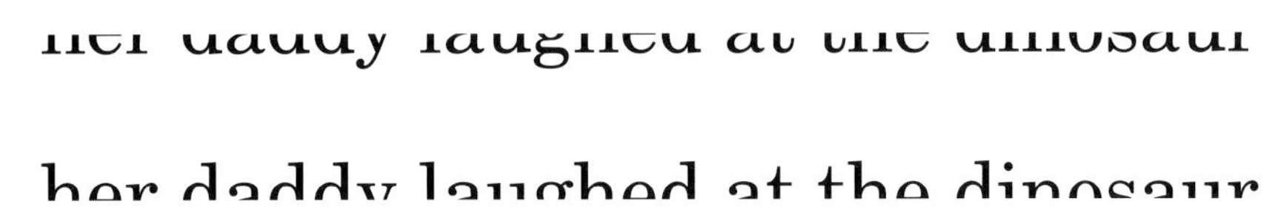

Figure 4.40 The profile of the top part of the letters is important for reading words.

Figure 4.41 In this typeface the o, a and g are very similar in shape.

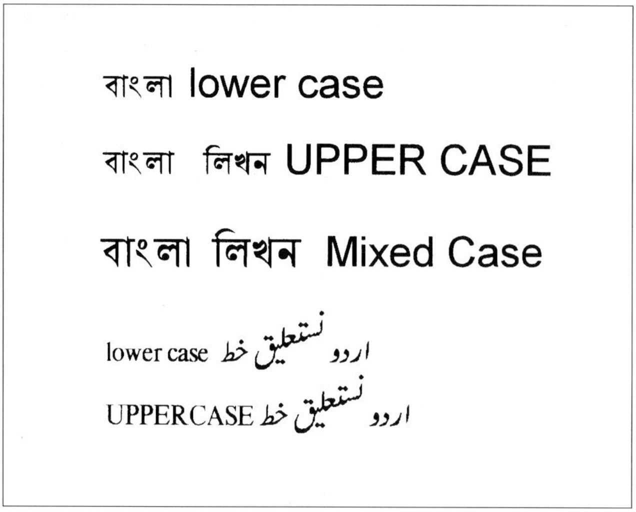

বাংলা lower case

বাংলা লিখন UPPER CASE

বাংলা লিখন Mixed Case

lower case خط نستعلیق اردو

UPPERCASE خط نستعلیق اردو

Figure 4.42 This illustration shows some of the problems of matching typefaces according to the same nominal size.

The top two examples show 16 point 'English' (a term used to describe the Latin version of a typeface in some programs that allow Latins to be combined with non-Latins) alongside 16 point Bengali. The Bengali appears much smaller, when matched against both lower-case and upper-case forms. A more appropriate match occurs when 22 point Bengali is used alongside 16 point English as in the third example.
Related, but different problems occur in the last two examples. Both 'English' and Urdu claim to be 16 point, although visually the English is much smaller than what would usually be regarded as 16 point.

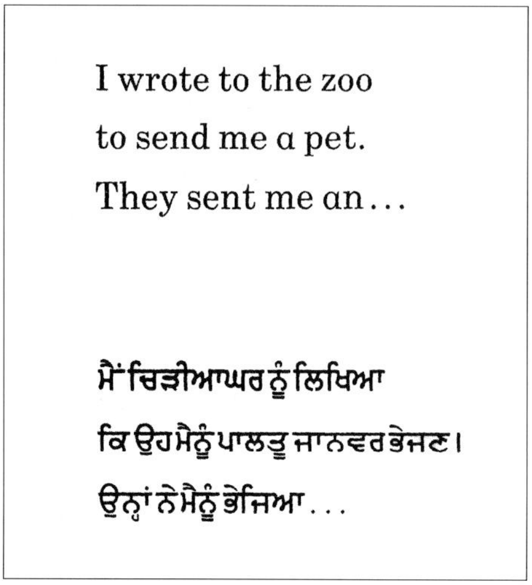

I wrote to the zoo
to send me a pet.
They sent me an ...

ਮੈਂ ਚਿੜੀਆਘਰ ਨੂੰ ਲਿਖਿਆ
ਕਿ ਉਹਮੈਨੂੰ ਪਾਲਤੂ ਜਾਨਵਰ ਭੇਜਣ।
ਉਨ੍ਹਾਂ ਨੇ ਮੈਨੂੰ ਭੇਜਿਆ ...

Figure 4.43 Detail from *Dear Zoo* by Rod Campbell. Panjabi translation: Amarjit Chandan. London: Ingham Yates Associates, 1987

In this example there is hardly any space between the words in the Panjabi version of the text.

of the Latin alphabet, typefaces suitable for children are likely to have the following characteristics:

- Tall ascenders that emphasize the word shape (Figure 4.40). Fluent readers don't read letter by letter; their eyes make a series of fixations across a line of type taking in several words at a time. Word shapes rather than individual letters are important, and it is the profile of the top part of the word that is particularly helpful in the reading process.
- A clear distinction between characters so they are not confused. In some typefaces o's, a's and g's can look very similar and this can cause confusion (Figure 4.41).

Typeface choice for non-Latin scripts is rather more problematic. Although there are many non-Latin types (see, for instance, Downie, 1963), these have been designed for high-level typesetting systems. Many publishers use various forms of desktop publishing to produce their books, and far fewer non-Latin typefaces have been produced for this process. What this means in practice is that there is much less choice: finding a non-Latin script that is appropriate for children could be quite difficult. Alison Black (1990) gives a full account of criteria for choosing typefaces for desktop publishing. Some of her discussion focusses on non-Latin typefaces and raises the following points:

- Typefaces of the same nominal size may not appear the same size, so a 14 point Bengali typeface may look significantly smaller than a 14 point Latin font (Figure 4.42).
- Non-Latin fonts for desktop publishing are likely to be available in a limited range of sizes only. When choosing type for dual texts, therefore, it is better to choose the non-Latin font and size first so that the Latin font can be matched to it.

2 Use of space

Careful use of space, so that the type is legible

and easy for children to read, is important. Walker (1993) summarizes the key issues and stresses that the relationship between the size of the letters and the space between the lines and the length of the line is critical. Generally, the larger the typesize, the longer the line length needs to be and the greater the distance between the lines. Space between lines is very important. If there isn't enough, children can lose their place, miss out lines or repeat them. Type which doesn't have enough space between the lines is very uninviting to read. This point was picked up by children in the fieldwork: the double-spread from *The enchanted palace* (see Figure 4.36) shows type that children found hard to read because the lines were too close together and too long.

3 Awareness of conventions

In some children's books we have noticed typographic mistakes that may have occurred because designers have been unaware of conventions of the non-Latin script concerned. In Figure 4.43, for example, the Panjabi text has been set without any significant space between words. Such mistakes not only hinder children's reading development, but also send out negative status messages. They also emphasize the importance of getting texts checked by people that are aware of publishing conventions in the language concerned and that have some awareness of the typographic factors that may help children to read.

What the fieldwork suggests

The fieldwork and resulting discussions in Project schools also drew attention to the following issues that are likely to be important in designing and producing dual texts.

1 Relationship between text and pictures

- There is a link between the arrangement of text and pictures and how a dual text is read and used. We saw, for example, how the design of *Sameep and the parrots* and *School dinners* (see Figures 4.21 and 4.22) affected both reading strategy and circumstances of use. Both these books are examples where text and pictures are in the same relative positions throughout. This, too, could be a design feature that is important: it could, for example, be very unsettling for beginner readers to have to search around for the text they have to read. Because dual texts have two languages presented on a page, they are graphically much more complex than children's books with just one language.
- Neither text should be obscured by illustrations because they become hard to read: only the very palest images should run behind text. Making a window in the illustration and putting text in it can be distracting because it destroys the completeness of the picture.

2 Status

- Status differences in typography and production are noticed and thought to be important by teachers and children.
- Consistency in the mode of writing is more important than, for instance, having both languages typeset. Handwriting for both languages could be appropriate as long as it is done well.
- Use of space should be consistent in both languages – if one language has generous interline space, the other language should have too.
- Space should be used so that pages have room to breathe: both languages need enough space around them to make them distinct from each other and from the pictures.
- Particular care should be taken when another language is added to an existing English text. The other language can seem less important if it is squashed in and if the action in the picture relates only to the English text.

Nearly every day Mummy reads to me. I try to read
as well. Mummy helps me.

લગભગ રોજ મમ્મી મને વાંચી સંભળાવે છે. હું પોતે પણ વાંચવાનો
પ્રયત્ન કરું છું. મમ્મી મને મદદ કરે છે.

Theory in practice

In the course of the Project we found many
examples of well-designed, popular dual
texts. The following are a few of those picked
out as such by our research team.

The English and Gujarati book *Me playing*
(Blackie & Son, 1987), shows relatively short
pieces of text that are both typeset and that
appear the same size (Figure 4.44). The only
way in which the English text could be said to
assume higher status is that it appears first.
However, the large amount of space around
each language gives emphasis to both. Rather
more text appears on the pages from *Shan
helps Rani* (André Deutsch, 1990). The treatment of both languages on each of the pages
illustrated is consistent: the typography of
both appears to have been carefully considered (Figure 4.45). Another good example is
Lights for Gita (Mantra, 1994): here the Urdu
text comes first and takes precedence on the
page therefore (Figure 4.46).

Back at home Shan and Mother waited
for Rani. She had been gone a long time.
"I'll see if she's coming," said Shan.
"A quick look, then," said Mother.

ਪਿਛੇ ਘਰ ਮਾਂ ਤੇ ਸ਼ਾਨ ਰਾਨੀ ਦੀ ਉਡੀਕ ਕਰਦੇ ਸਨ।
ਉਸਨੂੰ ਗਈ ਹੋਈ ਕਾਫ਼ੀ ਦੇਰ ਹੋ ਗਈ ਸੀ।
'ਮੈਂ ਵੇਖਦਾਂ ਕਿ ਉਹ ਆਂਦੀ ਪਈ ਹੈ ਕਿ ਨਹੀਂ,' ਸ਼ਾਨ ਨੇ
ਕਿਹਾ।
'ਛੇਤੀ ਜਹੀ ਝਾਤੀ ਮਾਰ ਫੇਰ,' ਮਾਂ ਨੇ ਕਿਹਾ।

a

Back at home Shan and Mother waited
for Rani. She had been gone a long time.
"I'll see if she's coming," said Shan.
"A quick look, then," said Mother.

گھر میں شان اور ماں رانی کا انتظار کر رہے تھے اسے گئے ہوئے کافی
دیر ہوگئی تھی۔ شان نے کہا میں دیکھتا ہوں، ہو سکتا ہے وہ آ رہی ہو جلدی
دیکھ کر آؤ ماں نے کہا۔

b

Back at home Shan and Mother waited
for Rani. She had been gone a long time.
"I'll see if she's coming," said Shan.
"A quick look, then," said Mother.

ઘર શાન અને અેની મમ્મી રાનીની રાહ જોતા હતા.
તણીને ગયે ઘણી વાર થઈ ગઈ હતી.
શાને કહ્યું, "તણી આવે છે કે કેમ હું તપાસ કરી
આવું."
મમ્મી બોલી, "ભલે જલ્દી જોઈ આવ."

c

There may, however, be some situations when different typographic treatment of the two languages is appropriate. Children and teachers in our fieldwork thought the typography in *The magic ink* was very clear. The Panjabi text, however, is bolder than the English. It may be that bilingual readers find this kind of graphic emphasis of the non-English text helpful. Another example of this convention is in *The first rains* (Mantra, 1984). Here, again, the Bengali is bolder and larger: the English appears the subsidiary language (Figure 4.47).

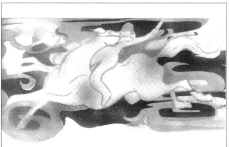

> Gently, Dad turned Gita towards the window. A large drop splashed against the glass. Then another and another.
> "It won't last long," said Gita, her voice wobbly.
> "The forecast says freezing rain tonight," said Dad. "Never mind. We'll have the fireworks tomorrow."
> "But I promised my friends..."

Figure 4.46 Detail from *Lights for Gita* by Rachel Gilmore, Urdu translation by Qamar Zamani. London: Mantra Publishing, 1994

The issue of directionality is best addressed when a dual text is designed as such from the outset. If Urdu is added to an existing text in English, it has to work within the conventions of the left–right opening book. *Send for Sohail* (Partnership Publishing, 1993) is an example of a dual text that deals successfully with the problem of directionality, incorporating English and Urdu texts with illustrations in a way that gives equal status to both languages (see Figure 4.39). Both languages are typeset and appear well-balanced in terms of size, weight and so on.

Our consideration of the design of dual texts has raised many interesting issues. It has shown that there are many ways of designing this kind of book, and that some ways of organizing text and pictures might be more effective than others. It has also shown that typography makes a difference and should be carefully considered.

> Dark clouds blackened the sky and then moved on. Arjuna thought they looked like warriors gathering in the mountains waiting to storm down with all their force.

Figure 4.47 A page from *The first rains* by Peter Bonnici, illlustrated by Lisa Kopper. London: Mantra Publishing Ltd, 1984

Emphasis is given to the Bengali text by its being bolder type than the English.

Translating children's books

The quality of translation is critical to the success of a book, whether in dual texts or in different language editions of the same book. Yet this is an issue which has received very little attention from monolingual teachers and publishers who tend to underestimate the complexity of the task. Various questions emerged as we started to look closely at translated texts, including:

- what makes a good translation?
- who is responsible for translation?
- what structures are in place to support the translator?
- how does the translator deal with novel situations, concepts or objects?
- do some topics make the journey between languages more successfully than others?

What makes a good translation?

Most teachers – whether monolingual or bilingual – agree that books in other languages are a useful classroom resource. This is an area, of course, where monolingual teachers are at a serious disadvantage because they cannot judge the quality of the translation. During our work on the Project we presented native speakers with a wide selection of translated texts. The consensus was that the quality of translation is very variable. Many minority parents and teachers have strong feelings on this subject. They argue that, while dual texts have a valuable educational role, their usefulness depends on how faithfully the translation mirrors the spirit of the original.

The complexities of translation have been taxing writers since the days of Cicero. The challenge is to transform a text from one language into another, retaining, as far as possible, the content, formal features and functions of the original. Important choices need to be made between word-for-word or literal translation and meaning-for-meaning or free translation. As Bell (1991) points out, the translator cannot win: literal translation is criticized for its ugliness; free translation for its inaccuracy. There is evidence of similar tensions around multilingual resources for children.

The people we consulted shared these concerns. Some were clearly irritated by obvious departures from the original text. *The Fox and the Crane* (Hounslow Community Language Service, 1990), for instance, tells how the Crane struggles to eat soup from a plate. In the Gujarati translation, Crane struggles to both 'eat soup' and 'drink soup' in the course of the same sentence. On other occasions, the translator has made what appears to be a careless mistake: the Panjabi version of *Soma goes to market* (Suhada Press, nd) translates 'He lives with his mother and Daddy and little sister Mina in a big *town*' as 'He lives with his mother and Daddy and little sister Mina in a big *room*.'

A more frequent criticism from native speakers is that, while translations are grammatically correct, they are stylistically flawed. Discussions of translated texts all too often provoke comments such as 'It doesn't sound good' or 'It sounds disjointed.' Sometimes erudite vocabulary and complex structures are used which make the translation far more difficult than the corresponding English text. This problem is often related to the sociolinguistic position of linguistic minority communities. For instance, many Moslem children speak Panjabi at home but study Urdu as the language of high culture. Similarly, many Italian children speak a southern Italian dialect but study standard Italian; and most Bangladeshi children speak Sylheti but study Bengali. For this reason, it is not unusual to find that a translator has chosen a word from the standard rather than the everyday language of the child: the use, for instance, of *bhojan* for dinner, rather than the more familiar *roti* , in the Panjabi translation of *School dinners.*

In books for beginners, the choice of an occasional word from the standard language is not too serious: it can sound very formal and stilted, but is unlikely to interfere with a child's understanding of the text, particularly where there are also visual cues. But, in books designed for more experienced readers, the decision to use words and grammatical structures outside the experience of young British readers can interrupt the flow. The use of highly literary and formal language makes the translation far more difficult to read than the original English.

While many parents are clear that they wish their children to learn the standard language as the language of high culture, community language teachers often express the view that it would be a more realistic educational goal to promote the language of the home as a bridge to the acquisition of the standard or official language (Alladina & Edwards, 1991).

It is also important to recognize that commercial considerations sometimes affect decisions about translation. If the target community is, say, Greek Cypriot, should the book be translated into the conservative Cypriot dialect spoken by the majority of Hellenophones in Britain, or into modern standard Greek? If publishers are hoping to reach a British market, it would make good sense to seek a Cypriot Greek translation; but, if they are hoping to reach an international audience (which might include Greek children learning English in Greece, or Greek Americans), modern standard Greek would be the obvious choice.

Who translates?

While small community publishing houses are sensitive to the issues raised by translation, the same level of awareness can't be assumed

for mainstream publishers. We have anecdotal evidence, for instance, of books being sent to agencies better geared to commercial than to educational translation. Those responsible for the translation may well have expertise in the language of advertising or technical and commercial documents, but little or no experience of the language of children's books.

It is widely believed that anyone who speaks another language is capable of translation. The reality, of course, is that quality translation is a highly skilled act of re-creation which faithfully mirrors the spirit of the original. Very few people are equipped to meet these demands. In the UK, for instance, most people are familiar with European languages like French and German, but knowledge of Indian and Asian languages has traditionally been limited to civil servants wishing to advance their careers in the colonial service. There is inevitably a shortage of professional translators in non-European languages, particularly translators with experience of children's literature. This places heavy responsibilities on publishers and others involved in translation to explore alternative ways of ensuring that the end product is of a high quality.

Who supports the translator?

Monolingual authors can rely on a high level of support in the form of editors and proof-readers. Translators don't usually have access to this kind of support. Monolingual mainstream publishers – like monolingual teachers – often have little sensitivity to multilingual matters. In the absence of an experienced editor and proof-reader, the translator is likely to be the sole arbiter of the end product and the only person to check the proofs. Under these circumstances, it is not surprising that serious errors occur. Chatterji (1991, p. 3) writes about a dual text with 'great chunks of text missing in the translation'.

Figure 4.48 Page from *Do you believe in magic?* by Saviour Pirotta, illustrated by Mrinal Mitra, Chinese translation by Sylvia Denham. London: Mantra Publishing Ltd, 1991

In the Chinese version of the text there is no reference to finding the shell on the beach at midnight: a proof-reading error, or not enough space for the full version in Chinese?

ਇਮਰਾਨ ਕੋਲ ਕਿੰਨੇ ਸਾਰੇ ਹੈਟ ਹਨ।
Imran has lots of hats to choose from.

Figure 4.49 Detail from *Getting dressed* by Kati Teague, Panjabi translation by Swaran Chandan. Hayes: Magi Publications, 1989

The word 'hat' has been transliterated even though 'topi' is a Panjabi word in everyday use.

On some occasions, decisions about translation may be affected by page layout. In Figure 4.48 the Chinese version reads:

> Sumed brought a seashell back from his holiday.
> 'This is a magic shell,' he says.

and makes no reference to finding the shell on the beach at midnight as in the English. It is difficult to know whether we are dealing here with a proof-reading error or whether the translator had made a deliberate decision to shorten the text to achieve a visual balance on the page.

Dealing with new situations

When translators have to deal with situations, concepts or objects which do not exist in the country of origin the most frequent solution is to transliterate the English word. For instance, in *A day at ...* (Ealing Education Department, nd) 'number work' and 'apparatus' are transliterated into Urdu script, while the Panjabi version of *Prince Cinders* (Magi Publications, 1993) transliterates *chimney* into Gurmukhi script. By and large, this seems to work well as a translation strategy, although unfamiliarity with an aspect of English language or culture occasionally results in a transliteration which is not faithful to the original. In the Gujarati version of *A wet dinner-time,* (Cambridge University Press and Jennie Ingham Associates, 1989) for instance, the girl's name, Ginny, is transliterated as [gɪni] and not [dʒɪni]. There was also a feeling among the people we consulted that this strategy was overused. They pointed to examples such as the transliteration of 'hat' in *Getting dressed* by Kati Teague (Magi, 1989) when the Panjabi word 'topi' is in everyday use (Figure 4.49).

Transliteration is a more difficult option, however, in a writing system like Chinese. In order to transliterate, you have to find a character which is close to the sound in question

Quick, Spot, follow me!

快點，小波，
跟隨着我！

Figure 4.50 Page from *Spot goes to the farm* by Eric Hill. London: Roy Yates Books, 1989

and this is often problematic. Take, for instance, the attempt by the translator of *Do you believe in magic?* to transliterate the name *Wicks*. The character selected, pronounced as /wik/ in Cantonese, is a technical term for frontier or region and not a name. Although the sound match is a good one, it is unlikely that children will recognize this character.

This same problem seems to have engaged Chinese translators of the ubiquitous *Spot* books. In early publications, 'Spot' is transliterated as *shibode*; in later publications, the transliteration has been replaced with *xiao bo* – Little Bo. This attempt is far more successful: the use of 'little' and two syllables makes it sound a more authentic Chinese name, and 'Bo' does not depart too dramatically from 'Spot' (Figure 4.50).

Cultural relevance

An increasing number of dual texts are adaptations of original monolingual English books. However, different books make the journey from one language to another with varying degrees of success. Certain themes appear to work much better than others. The universality of traditional folk and fairy tales

makes them a particularly popular choice. Animal stories also tend to travel well, as do stories about everyday experiences. It is important, though, that these everyday experiences should be common to all readers, monolingual and bilingual. The following extract is from *After dark* (Magi, 1989):

> By now, Anna had curled up contentedly, asleep. But not Martha. She's thinking about Mummy and Daddy getting dressed up for a night out. They look happy. But the night is still scary.

In cultures where children are not excluded from adult social activities, the notion of Mummy and Daddy getting dressed up for a night out will seem strange. Nor should we minimize the impact of this strangeness. *Bibi and the little bird* (Hong Kong: Arts Publishing Co., 1984, pp. 2–11), a moral tale in Chinese and English designed to encourage toilet training, gives the monolingual English speaker a useful insight into how it feels to be faced with culturally inappropriate material:

> The birds are singing sweetly on the tree. Bibi and his friends are playing happily under the tree.
> Bibi is too fond of playing and doesn't go to the toilet when he is eager to make water.
> He is not ashamed of making water freely at any place.
> A little bird follows Bibi's bad example. It flies and loosens the bowels.
> The little bird's bowels fall precisely on Bibi's face. Take a smell, it is very, very stinking.
> His friend brings a towel and helps Bibi wash his face clean.
> Pointing to the bird, the children shout, 'Little bird, Little bird. Don't discharge night soil and urine freely at any place any more.' Bibi keeps silent. He turns round and steals a glance. Bibi says to the Little bird gently, 'Let's not discharge night soil and urine freely at any place. O.K.'

Closely related to the question of the cultural relevance of the text is the handling of visual images. Many Chinese readers perceive illustrations in books on Chinese themes as lacking authenticity, the imperfect European interpretation of Chinese art. A similar problem can be found in books portraying Indian and Pakistani families. Teachers from these communities consulted during the Project pointed out that items of clothing like sarees were sometimes the only features which distinguished South Asian characters from whites. They also objected to the cartoon representation of minority children. Cartoons are caricatures. While it may be acceptable to use them to represent the dominant group in society, the fact that they may emphasize negative stereotypes of minorities raises uncomfortable questions.

New directions

For the moment, most publishing in community languages involves translation from English to another language. This pattern may well change. And, as confidence within minority communities grows, we may also see a move towards bilingual writers producing books in both their languages. This is already the case in multilingual countries like India where children's authors like Ira Saxena write in both English and Hindi. Significantly, she describes the task of producing the second language version as being like writing a new book, with no hint of mechanical translation. The issues involved in producing a faithful equivalent are the same, of course, whoever the translator and whatever the direction of the translation.

Summary

What makes a good translation?

• Publishers need to recognize that speaking another language is not the only qualification for being a good translator of children's books.
• Translators need to have first-hand experience of children who speak the community language in question. They should be familiar with children's literature in English and the community language.
• The translation also needs to be tested in co-operation with children and community language teachers. This kind of consultation will help avoid the pitfalls of language being too formal or literary and will ensure that the translation is of the same level of difficulty as the original text.
• Publishers have a responsibility to provide the same level of support to translators as they offer to writers in English. This includes access to copy-editing and proofreading.
• Publishers also have a responsibility for choosing wisely the titles which will be translated. Some themes work much better in some cultural contexts than others.

5 Writing as a resource

Some teachers assume that their sole responsibility is for teaching children to read – and write – in English, and that other languages have no part to play in this process. However, our understanding of the ways we learn has greatly expanded in recent years. It is much clearer now that the cognitive skills associated with literacy are not acquired separately in different languages. Learning which has taken place, for instance, in Panjabi is readily transferred to English or other language learning situations. Increasing numbers of teachers view opportunities for writing in other languages as an important way to consolidate and extend children's competencies, and not as an obstacle to acquiring skills in English.

The teaching of writing works best when children belong to communities of writers (Graves, 1983; Gregory *et al.* 1991): teachers writing alongside children in writers' workshop activities; older children writing for younger children; parents writing for children and so on. There is every reason to suppose that this approach will work irrespective of the language. Bilingual teachers are extremely well-placed to support children's writing in other languages; monolingual teachers can draw on the skills of colleagues, parents and other experienced bilingual writers.

Bilingual teachers have an important complementary role as authors in their own right. They are frequently called upon to produce their own resources with the needs of a specific audience in mind and to address obvious gaps in classroom materials.

Support for writing in other languages

Most children's first experience of writing in the community language is in the home. It usually centres around parents – most often mothers – and older siblings. Many of the bilingual children we talked to in mainstream schools also attended community classes or, occasionally, had a private tutor. Learning to write in the community language, then, is a high status activity.

Monolingual teachers are unsure as to how best to foster children's writing skills: 'Who will read what they write and who will understand?' Teachers also expressed concern about their inability to help when children make mistakes. This worry is misplaced. It is possible, for instance, to call upon a range of bilingual adults for help. Nor should we forget that mistakes are a natural part of the learning process, irrespective of the language in question. While corrective feedback is important and can only be provided by native speakers, monolingual teachers can none the less show bilingual children that their efforts are valued and provide a range of reasons and audiences for writing in two languages. As the head-teacher of Thomas Buxton Junior School reflected:

> I was watching a boy in one of the top classes who writes Bengali absolutely fluently. He had written a story about three pages long in Bengali and was writing it in English as well. He is completely bilingual – his mother has been teaching him. We can't do that ourselves, but where it happens, we must be supportive.

Some children will be able to work on their own. They may be able to undertake more extended writing which can be 'published' in books for sharing with other children in the class or for wider distribution through the school library. However, the time required to

become efficient writers means that very few children have the necessary skills to work independently on either dual language or single language stories. They may therefore need to write in collaboration with more experienced peers or with the help of bilingual adults. If they do not have the stamina to produce more extended writing, they can be encouraged to produce short pieces for a classroom display or the school magazine, or contribute to a collection of class stories on a similar theme. Figures 5.1– 5.3 show how handwritten stories illustrated with children's line drawings can be very effective.

Figure 5.3 Handmade books at Thomas Buxton Junior School

Figures 5.1 and 5.2 Dual texts written and illustrated by children at Cranford Infant School

Handwriting in other languages

As Sampson (1985, p. 21) points out:

> ... *a script is only a device for making examples of a language visible*; the script is not itself the language. One language may be written in different scripts, and the same script may be used to write different languages.

The presence of different languages – and scripts – in the classroom provides many opportunities for reflecting on the different solutions for making language visible. A pupil at the Brent Indian Association classes explained this in terms of 'English is abc, but Gujarati is a different kind of writing. You have to do funny letters'. The differences, though, can also be a source of pleasure. As a Pakistani girl pointed out, 'I enjoy writing Urdu because it looks so different.'

Children need support in developing the graphic skills of handwriting and word processing. Before they can express themselves in another language they have to become familiar with the script and writing system of that language. They need to learn individual characters and how these combine in larger units, as well as learning the writing conventions of a particular script: use of space, punctuation, formal and informal styles and so on.

All the Project languages use non-Latin scripts which offer all children many exciting opportunities for learning about writing systems. Two of these languages have writing systems that are very different from the English alphabetic one. Chinese, for example, is a logographic system where each character or graph represents a word or part of a word. This means that the Chinese writing system is made up of thousands of graphs. Urdu, written in Nastaliq (the preferred form) Naksh script, uses a largely consonantal system which doesn't have letters for all vowels. The vowels which are not written in full can be marked by diacritics above or below the consonant letters, but are often omitted.

There are also many differences to do with the ways scripts are organized: how characters are written within a line, character variants, directionality, use of space and so on.

Writing on the line?

Children learning to write in English have to learn about the relationship of letters to a baseline: some letters sit on it, some extend below. Devanagari script and those based on it, for example, for writing Panjabi and Bengali, has letters hanging from a top line (Figure 5.4).

Chinese graphs are constructed within a notional square. Figure 5.5 shows a page from a copybook published in 1990: each large square is subdivided into nine small ones, and the strokes of the character are placed in relation to these. As confidence increases, the child moves on to paper divided into squares without the subdivisions.

In children's exercise books for learning to write Nastaliq script the characters are placed between a top line and a baseline. This space is divided into six segments, and each character has a place between the top and base lines which may vary according to its position within a word.(Figure 5.6).

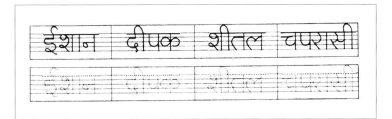

Figure 5.4 Detail from Hindi copybook showing how characters hang from a top line.

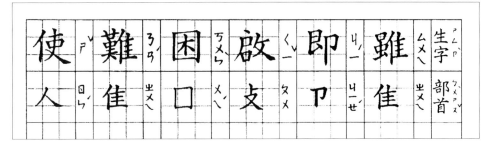

Figure 5.5 Page from *Exercise book for Chinese* (trans.), Hong Kong, 1990

Chinese characters are written in relation to a notional square. Here the square is subdivided into nine so that beginners can learn the correct proportion of each stroke in relation to the others that make up the word.
The second row shows the root of the word in the first row.

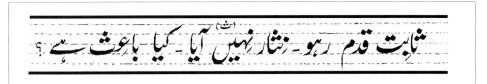

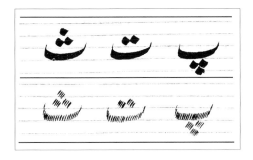

Figure 5.6 Details from Nastaliq copybooks *Urdu beautiful writing* (Urdu Khush Khati), Lahore & Islamabad, nd

The example on the left shows individual characters placed on a five-line horizontal grid. The shading shows the angle of the nib and how this affects the width of the strokes.
The top example shows characters in context and their relationship within the writing line.

Figure 5.7 Examples from Gujarati copy-books

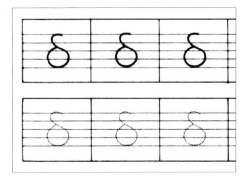

In Gujarati, children learn to write within a set of tramlines. Like Urdu, character shapes have their place within horizontal segments of the lines. In the examples illustrated in Figure 5.7, the first book has more segments than the second, and deals with individual letters rather than words.

Character sets

Some scripts have a very wide range of characters. In Latin script this range is relatively small. Children learn two variants of each letter – the capital and small letter forms. Indian and Pakistani scripts do not use capital letters, but do make use of a large number of character variants. In Nastaliq script, for example, the forms of the letters differ according to their position in a word: when standing alone, when final (joining the preceding form), when medial (joined to the preceding and following letters) and when initial (joined to succeeding letters) (Figure 5.8). Some scripts, such as Bengali and Gujarati, make use of a large number of conjunct characters (those formed by the combination of two or more others). Usually the shape of the conjunct is related to the characters that are combined, but sometimes this relationship is hard to see (Figure 5.9).

All the Project scripts have a larger (and, in the case of Chinese, much larger) set of characters than English and this strongly influences the way handwriting is taught. Learning Chinese and South-Asian scripts requires careful copying of character shapes as well as memorizing the shape of each character. In the case of Chinese, for example, learning how to form the characters and then memorizing them takes a long time. Children have to acquire a large stock of characters before they can use them creatively. Wong (1991, p. 200) describes the process thus:

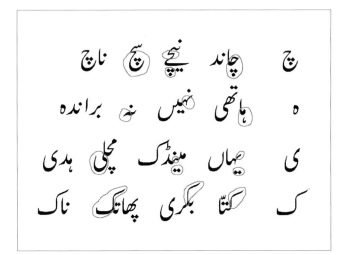

Figure 5.8 This illustration shows how the shape of four Urdu characters (che, hey, choti ye and kaaf) changes according to position in the word. The tinted areas areas show the character in initial, medial, final and isolated forms.

Figure 5.9 Examples of conjunct characters in Bengali. The left-hand column shows characters side by side; the right-hand one shows the conjunct form.

Younger children are taught how to write the various strokes – lines, sweeps, angles and hooks ... and the basic sequence (left to right, top to bottom, etc.) [see fig 5.10] of putting all the strokes together to form a Chinese character. Most Chinese children get the sequence confused [see fig 5.11]. After students have acquired a certain number of words, they will be taught to make sentences with the words they have learned. From the ages of 10 or 11 they will be required to write short essays and family letters.

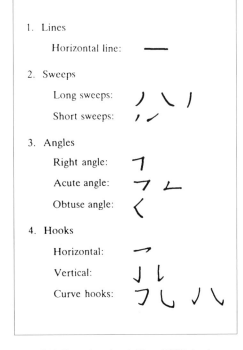

Figure 5.10 Illustrations given in Wong (1991) showing above the basic strokes of Chinese characters and on the left, the proper and then the improper sequence of strokes to make the Chinese character for 'field'.

Proper sequence

|	冖	⊐	冊	田
1. Vertical line	2. Right angle	3. Horizontal line	4. Vertical line	5. Horizontal line

Improper sequence

|	冖	⊐	⊟	田
1. Vertical line	2. Right angle	3. Horizontal line	4. Horizontal line	5. Vertical line

(*Mistake*: Steps 4 and 5 have been reversed.)

There is also an element of careful copying for children learning to write South Asian languages. Although the placing of diacritics in Indian languages presents problems for children, there are fewer elements of the script to learn than in Chinese. A seven-year-old at Barham Primary described to us how she was learning to write in Gujarati: 'I look at the book first. We have Gujarati Learning Books from Bombay. Then I close it and try to write the words.' A nine-year-old talked of the importance in Panjabi of the 'lines and dots and the dash – that's like a full stop. You have to be careful the way you write. If you aren't, the person can't read the thing.'

As was the case for reading, more experienced children acknowledged that writing gets easier as you go along. There was some disagreement between different language groups, however, as to which activity is more demanding: reading or writing. Many speakers of South Asian languages felt that writing is more difficult, but children from the Chinese community felt that reading provided even greater challenges than writing. Michael, a seven-year-old at Barham Primary, explained that, although he had a book for writing Chinese, he wasn't 'ready to read it yet'. Ten-year-old Andrew, a student at the Hounslow Chinese School, made a similar point: 'It's OK writing in Chinese, because we have to revise for a test. Reading is harder.'

Handwriting skills are acquired through constant practice and without this children are unlikely to make rapid progress. Children also pointed to the difficulties of having few opportunities to practise. A six-year-old at Ramgarhia Sabha Sunday School explained this problem thus:

> I find long words hard. It's hard for me because one day I go to Panjabi and Monday, Tuesday, Wednesday, Thursday, Friday I go to English school, so I sometimes forget.

Teachers we spoke to pointed out that there is an enormous range of competencies, but that the only children who reach high standards are those who have been to school in the country of origin. There is simply not the time nor the expertise in most mainstream classrooms to allow children to become biliterate. Those children who do achieve high standards have considerable support from community schools, parents or both. Given the very real practical difficulties, the best that teachers can hope to achieve is an atmosphere which acknowledges and encourages children's efforts outside school.

Opportunities for experimenting with other scripts should not, of course, be restricted to bilingual children. Many monolingual children are fascinated by different writing systems; bilingual peers are usually very willing teachers, as shown in the following case study from Redlands Primary.

Case study: nameplates in Nastaliq

Interesting work on Islamic calligraphy and design grew spontaneously from a project on writing and communication with 10- and 11-year-olds at Redlands Primary School, Reading. The class teacher, Elizabeth Pye, had linked the history of different alphabets with different holy books. Children compared different versions of the Bible and brought in copies of the Qu'rān from home. They had also experimented with a range of different writing tools and materials, including Chinese brushes and ink blocks.

As part of the project, children had been asked to designname plates using templates with a repeating eight-point star shape as a border. Islamic patterns were part of the cultural tradition of Pakistani and other Moslem children, but every member of the class had been exposed to Islamic art through tiles and pictures of mosques; they also had experience of colouring Islamic patterns as part of their exploration of shape and space in maths.

By chance, Asya, a sixteen-year-old Pakistani girl and former pupil, arrived for a week's work experience at the school when the class was working on this project. One of the children asked Asya to write their name in Nastaliq script as the centrepoint of their design. Asya duly pencilled in the name for them to trace over and was soon responding to other requests for help. The exercise generated a great deal of discussion and interest in calligraphy. Alice, for instance, said she liked the style of writing: 'It was a new experience. It was fancy and decorative and I liked the way it flowed.' The end products were certainly impressive.

'Catherine' and 'Francesca' in Nastaliq script

Word-processing in other languages

Word-processing is another way multilingual writing can be brought into the classroom. Word processors also provide teachers with a cheap and semi-professional way of producing multilingual resources.

Multilingual software is found in growing numbers of schools but is still not widespread. For instance, two of the mainstream schools included in the Project had no facility of this kind; the third had the equipment for teachers to produce multilingual teaching materials, but no access for classroom use; while, in the fourth, teachers, children and parents made extensive use of multilingual software.

None of the community schools had computers, although teachers at the Ramgarhia Sabha Sunday School had access to a computer at the Gurdwara. Several teachers, however, said they used word-processing software in other languages at home to produce resources for school. As a teacher in the Hounslow Chinese School pointed out:

> As voluntary schools we have to be realistic. Most schools don't even have enough textbooks, never mind computers. It's something for the future.

Although multilingual word-processing in UK schools is still in the early stages, there have been some important recent developments. The Multilingual Word-processing Project, for instance, introduced software for a range of community languages into three outer-London education authorities (NCET, 1992). This project aimed to support the teaching of community languages by using word processors as tools for developing materials and training for teachers. As part of another interesting project – Parents, Allwrite and Languages (PAL) – staff from the Inner London Educational Computing Centre offered word-processing training in local schools for parents and others from minority language communities. The products of this co-operation were stories, signs and labels in a variety of languages.

There are obvious difficulties with initiatives of this kind: parents sometimes feel insecure about their literacy skills, and teachers often fail to realize that translation is a highly skilled activity. None the less, teachers are encouraged to see the multilingual skills of members of minority communities as an invaluable resource for curriculum development and a means of involving parents in school activities. It also builds bridges to parents. Abbott (1994b) tells of a Gujarati father who already used a computer, but came to school for training in multilingual word-processing.

> Intending to stay for only an hour or so, he kept writing all morning and returned for the afternoon session. Eventually he printed out the text, rolled it up and tied it with a ribbon to take home to his wife. It was a lengthy, poetical declaration of his love for her and quite unlike the texts being created around him. For him, though, the school is now a different kind of place; not just an educational environment for his children but a support for his own literacy.

Using word processors in the classroom

Word-processing removes much of the anxiety associated with writing, allowing children to experiment with words: editing is quick and easy; spelling mistakes can be corrected with a few keystrokes; sections can be cut and pasted with minimal effort. These benefits apply, regardless of the language of the writer. Teachers and advisors involved in the NCET project, for example, were enthusiastic about the potential of word-processing for helping the writing development of bilingual children in both languages. Gulshan Kayembe (1992) tells how Kalpana, who had come to London as a seven-year-old from India, was, by the age of ten, confidently using a word processor to write poetry and stories in Gujarati, which she then translated into English.

This kind of multilingual word-processing helped to raise the status of community languages in the eyes of both monolingual and bilingual speakers. Shobhana Devani (1992) describes how, over the course of the project:

> The Gujarati children were gaining a tremendous sense of pride in their language and culture. I came across many Gujarati children of all ages who were not very happy to talk in their own language for fear of being ridiculed. Seeing their own script displayed on the screen validated their language and gave them confidence to use it. I found that it also generated interest in many monolingual children; many times they came to me and asked, 'Miss, can I learn how to write that?' or 'Can you teach me to talk and write that language?' To me, this change in attitude is very significant for multicultural education. IT, used in this way, is helping all children to recognise, value and appreciate linguistic and cultural diversity within our society.

The needs of children using a word processor to produce their own writing are different from those of teachers or publishers using word-processing software to produce reading materials. Children need a word processor that is easy to use and that offers opportunity to play with their own and other languages. Teachers using word processors to produce resources for use in class may have different requirements, such as production quality (well-drawn characters, and a facility to change size and boldness), and, if producing dual texts, the ability to combine English and non-Latin scripts in the same document.

There are a number of guides to multilingual word-processing for PC and Macintosh (eg Raby, 1991a; Ganly, Gilding & Green, 1991)

which list the software available for word-processing in a range of languages using non-Latin scripts. The range is somewhat overwhelming at first glance, but in practice choice is narrowed down by looking at what will run on your computer, how much you can afford and what you need the multilingual application for. These and other issues are discussed by Raby (1991b).

Making software accessible to children

Having software is one thing, making it easy for children to use is another. Some concern was expressed by both teachers and children about the difficulty of word-processing in other languages.

Some of the difficulty children face is because the Project languages use scripts with large character sets (see examples of variants and conjuncts on pages 88 and 89). Word-processing programs for writing Urdu in Nastaliq tend to be expensive, and even these are unable to achieve the calligraphic qualities and beauty of the handwritten form. To cope with the large number of variant forms, most programs that use Nastaliq have 'contextual analysis' which means that the correct character variant for its position in the word automatically appears as the word is typed. The advantage of this is that all character variants are held on a single shift keyboard: the operator types the character required and sees the cursor moving backwards and forwards along a line of type inserting, deleting and altering characters according to their position in a word. Writing Urdu without contextual analysis is more complicated because you have to know which variant form you need before you type it, and then search through levels of shift on the keyboard to find the character. Most programs used in schools don't have contextual analysis, and knowing which variant form is needed and where to find it on the keyboard makes considerable demands on the children.

A similar feature to contextual analysis is 'automatic conjuncting'. This occurs in the more expensive programs for writing languages that use a lot of conjunct characters (eg Bengali and Gujarati). It means that the conjunct form is generated automatically when a 'conjuncting key' is pressed between the two characters that are conjoined. On cheaper programs the conjunct characters are found through levels of shift. With automatic conjuncting you need to know which characters to conjunct and then instruct the program.

Children and teachers at Thomas Buxton expressed frustration over their experience of word-processing in Bengali. Nine-year-old

Zahada talked of the difficulty of using the keyboard: 'It's not that easy – you can't find the letters. You have to look for the letters on the keyboard'. Headteacher, Wanda Garland, confirmed this was the case: 'It takes a long time to do Bengali word-processing on the computer'. Community language teachers, however, report that the repetition and effort involved in producing conjuncts by a variety of key combinations can be very effective in helping children to learn these letter shapes.

There have been some attempts, however, to make computing child-friendly. Though slow and frustrating to use, Allwrite has been designed with users in mind. The on-screen keyboard is very attractive to inexperienced users (see, for example, Viv Wheatley's (1991) account of using Allwrite with nursery children). The alphabet appears on the lower half of the screen, leaving space for the child's own writing (Figure 5.11). Characters can be selected using a mouse as well as a keyboard.

Using concept keyboards with bilingual overlays has proved a very successful way of introducing computers to children with a limited command of English. A concept keyboard is a plastic touch-sensitive tray, A3 or A4 in size, which connects to the computer and can be used as an alternative to the standard keyboard. It has 128 segments, each of which can be assigned its own function in the form of a word, a sentence, a number or a picture. Alternatively, the segments can be used in blocks. The usefulness for bilingual pupils is that overlays in community languages can be placed on the keyboard. Children press a key or a combination to produce words or sentences on the screen. However, concept keyboards can generate sentences only in languages which share the same word order as English.

Figure 5.11 Allwrite keyboard and screen for Panjabi.

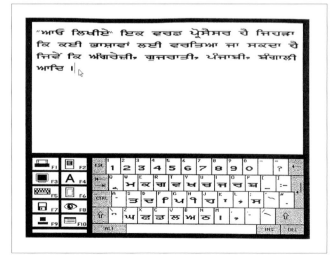

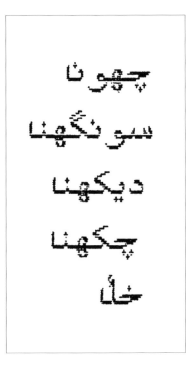

Figure 5.12 An example of character confusion at low resolution. In these Urdu examples there is danger that the final character may be mispronounced. The final stroke should be taller to avoid this confusion.

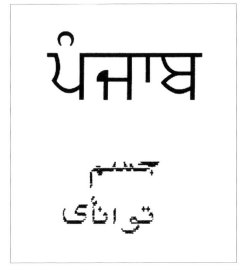

Character design

It might seem reasonable to expect characters produced by multilingual word-processing packages to be correct , but this isn't always the case. Part of the reason is the way fonts are designed: for many of the cheaper fonts the emphasis is on making a script available for a word processor rather than on producing a high-quality product. This sometimes results in less-than-perfect character shapes and in letters that are easily confused (Figure 5.12). Sometimes character sets are designed by people who do not know the languages concerned, or who have little experience in character design.

Some character design programs, for example, allow language 'experts' to colour in squares to make character shapes. The output of this procedure is very crude especially when compared with that from specialist type manufacturers. Resolution of output is also a factor in final character shape. Fine details are lost on low-resolution printers (Figure 5.13). This may result in two similar characters looking identical, and also presents problems for languages with diacritics. Many Asian letterforms are more complex in shape than English ones, and therefore perform less well at lower resolution. The educational advantages of word-processing in other languages may outweigh these disadvantages, but it is important to remember that the lower resolution may send messages about the status of the language when used alongside English. (The problem of status in dual texts is an issue discussed earlier, see pages 66–72.)

Figure 5.13 Examples of character definition from a high-resolution and a low-resolution output device.

Case study: a low-resolution Gujarati alphabet

Shobhana Devani designed the Gujarati character set for the Asian Folio multilingual word-processing package. This is an example of how a non-typographer can effectively design a low-resolution character set. Knowledge of the alphabet, the user group and the technical constraints imposed by the software allowed her to produce an appropriate, highly usable font. She describes the process thus:

I started by thinking about the layout of the keyboard and there were three options: correspondence to the QWERTY keyboard in sound; the Gujarati typewriter keyboard; or the sequence of the Gujarati alphabet. The Gujarati alphabet consists of 36 full letters, 20 half letters, 15 diacritical marks, 10 numerals, 6 conjunct letters, 9 punctuation and 6 mathematical signs, a total of 102. Since the BBC keyboard had only 94 keys, I included the most frequently used characters and accents. The ones that were omitted could be added by hand. The Folio keyboard layout broadly follows the Gujarati keyboard layout.

The Folio programme had the facility to design graphically each individual letter and accent on screen. It took me about four months to design the set of fonts I found acceptable. A plastic keyboard overlay was designed and each letter was cut and pasted on the overlay.

After six months I piloted the alphabet in two Brent Schools; one primary with a monolingual class teacher and one secondary school where Gujarati was taught as a curriculum subject.

The Gujarati children's reaction was one of wonder and surprise: Kalpana's first words to her teacher were, 'Look, Miss, it is my language on the computer.' Monolingual children showed a great deal of interest and many wanted to learn the 'secret' language.

As knowledge of the Gujarati alphabet was necessary for the use of Folio, we invited a Gujarati-speaking mother to come and help the monolingual teacher. We had some very interesting and original stories that had been part of 'grandmother's stories' tradition.

The response to this project was excellent. Children in all three schools wrote stories, poems, self-portraits, cooking recipes. They translated stories from Gujarati, labelled areas and displays in the classrooms. They wrote letters to parents and grandparents in India and attracted parents to come and help in the classrooms. The Gujarati-speaking teacher used it to create concept keyboard overlays. The software has also been used to create dual language books.

Example of Gujarati script using Folio fonts

નવુ મંદીર
પહેલા મંદીરની જગ્યાએ ચર્ચ હતુ.
પછી માણસો ભાંગી નાખ્યો ૧૯૮૫ માં કેમકે માણસોને સારુ નતુ
લાગતુ. પછી પુજારી નવા મકાનમાં ભગવાનને પધારયા. પછી નવુ
મંદીર કરતા કરતા ત્રણ વરશ થઈ ગયા.
અને હવે બધાં ત્યા પ્રાર્થના કરવા આવે છે.

Producing low-budget resources

Bilingual teachers, either working individually or as part of community language teaching teams, are often involved in producing multi-lingual learning resources. Such initiatives are many and varied: illustrated vocabulary lists to accompany work on different areas of the curriculum; translations of favourite stories pasted into existing single language books; original dual texts derived from children's stories; class worksheets; booklets for use by colleagues and children. These resources can be used within schools, or may be produced by support teams for wider circulation within the LEA or school board (a useful source of information on low-budget resources is the AIMER database, housed at the Reading and Language Information Centre at the University of Reading).

Such materials serve a valuable purpose for both pupils and teachers. Pupils have access to a wider range of books and games, allowing them to consolidate skills in their own community languages and acting as a valuable transition to English. Teachers involved in materials production have the chance to reflect more critically on the aims and content of their teaching. In most cases, the resulting books are eminently practical responses to the shortage of suitable teaching resources. They are, inevitably, produced on very low budgets and tend to be printed on cheap paper, using one-colour line drawings with text which is handwritten or produced on a typewriter or low-resolution word-processor.

One advantage that teachers have is that they know their audience and are likely to be familiar with the circumstances in which the document will be used. Throughout the Project we have seen many examples of teachers, writers, translators and designers working together to produce well-focussed materials. Hounslow Primary Language Service springs to mind as a producer of materials that have been made with the needs of users in mind.

When people work together to produce materials they have to give some thought to the roles and responsibilities they have to address in the process of document production. This process is just as much to do with design as is page layout and choice of typeface – if the design process is carefully considered there is a good chance that an appropriate, well-focussed document will result. There are many stages and roles involved in producing a book, as shown in the table below:

Roles	Responsibilities
project manager	making sure everything happens on time
writer	writing re-writing deciding what to illustrate
illustrator	doing the pictures/finding suitable pictures
editor	redrafting checking consistency in spelling, punctuation, grammar
designer	overall design scheme: planning pages, text typography, cover design formatting pages
typesetter	keying in text (sometimes done by the author)
proof reader	checking text is accurate
printer	producing multiple copies

Table 5.1 Stages and roles in producing a book

In traditional publishing, such roles were usually fulfilled by different people; with desktop publishing there is often less of a clear distinction between them, and sometimes stages are forgotten.

Making materials

All document production involves a number of stages: planning, editing, designing and so on. Producing materials such as dual texts or storybooks in languages other than English raises other issues, including translation, transliteration, and choice of production mode for non-Latin scripts.

As part of the Project we visited Hounslow Language Service. Hounslow is a vibrant multilingual community to the west of London. The largest minority groups are Sikh and Moslem Panjabi speakers who first came to England either from the Panjab or via the East African countries of Kenya, Uganda and Tanzania. The Hounslow Language Service provides support for bilingual learners both in English and in their other languages. It consists of over forty teachers, forty per cent of whom are bilingual. Materials production is an important area of work for the Language Service and designated teachers are responsible for areas such as Panjabi language support and bilingual word-processing.

To illustrate the various stages involved in producing documents the checklist below raises various issues and shows how the Hounslow team addresses some of them.

Planning

• What kind of materials need to be produced?
• Who are the readers and how are they going to use the book/worksheet etc?
• How are the materials going to be produced?

• Who is the production team and what are their responsibilities?

Bilingual materials in Hounslow are generally produced in response to varied requests from schools. Recent initiatives include materials which have grown out of a project offering advice to parents on reading; resources to support national curriculum assessment books; and vocabulary lists on different classroom topics. At the time of our visit, we observed bilingual language assistants involved in a workshop to produce materials on science vocabulary selected by mainstream teachers.

Language

• Who is responsible for translation?
• Is the translation appropriate for the readers?
• What about dialect variation?
• Is the text consistent in spelling, punctuation, grammar?
• If the text is a dual text, how does the translation reflect the original – does it relate to the same reading age?
• When is transliteration appropriate and what are the problems it raises?
• What provision is there for translations or transliterations to be tested on users?

Dialect variation is a particular concern for the Hounslow team. Their policy is to provide the standard form of a language but to acknowledge dialect differences and discuss these openly with children. Thus the standard Urdu word for white [səfed] might be used, but provoke comment from children who would be more likely to use [tʃɪtɑ] in their own speech. Standardization across languages raises similar issues. Decisions need to be made, for instance, as to whether 'book' should be translated as [kətɑb], the form normally used in both Urdu and everyday Panjabi, or [pʊstɑk], the Panjabi alternative which is considered 'purer' and 'more educated'. Occasionally, when there is no consensus, assistants seek advice from outside experts.

Transliteration is used as a matter of course in producing materials such as vocabulary lists. Although beginners in English may not know a term like 'energy', they may well understand this concept in their other language. Transliteration makes it possible for monolingual teachers to cue the meaning of a word for children who can't read the community language. It is also a useful tool for bilingual children whose spoken skills in the community language outstrip their literacy skills. However, it isn't always easy to find an acceptable transliteration and attempts are usually tested on readers who don't know the language in question.

Design issues

Getting things to look right is a skilled job. Most publishers employ designers who make decisions about typography and page organization. In school, handwriting may be the only means of producing text available, the word processor may have only one typeface that you can use and so on. Such constraints, however, need not stand in the way of typography that works and page layouts that are appropriate for the users. The issues that need to be considered when producing documents in school are summarized by Walker (1993) and include page layout, margins, typefaces and making type easy to read.
• Does the page layout support the way the book is going to be used?
• Does the typographic treatment of one language in a dual text, for example, make it appear more important than the other?
• Have the page designs been tried out on readers?

Although Hounslow Language Service regularly uses multilingual software to produce materials in Panjabi, they identify word processing in Urdu as a particular problem. There are two kinds of Perso-Arabic script: Naskh, which is closest to Arabic, and Nastaliq, which is related to Farsi. The preferred script for Urdu is Nastaliq, but the multilingual word-processing program currently in use in Hounslow was based on an imperfect adaptation of Naskh which can give rise to misunderstanding. This complication, together with the poor quality output from the dot matrix printer, has led Urdu-speaking language assistants to prefer using handwriting for their translations.

In addition to materials produced by teachers, many schools encourage parents to write in other languages. The range of reasons for writing is impressive – from labelling to translating children's work to writing stories of their own. Bilingual parents can play an important role in the community of writers, drawing on their own experiences of people and events which have been important in their family life as the subject matter of stories for their children.

Summary

Writing resources

- Writing in other languages can be promoted by both monolingual and bilingual teachers to value and acknowledge children's linguistic competencies.
- Writing provides a useful link with reading in other languages; and can encourage an awareness of other scripts and writing systems.
- The limited time and expertise in mainstream classrooms means that most literacy learning in other languages will take place in the home and the community.
- There are, however, many opportunities for children to develop their writing in community languages in mainstream schools. They can be encouraged to develop their writing in other languages for a variety of purposes and audiences. In some cases, they will be able to work independently; more often, though, they will need to write in collaboration with a more experienced peer or a bilingual adult.
- Handwriting and calligraphy provide valuable insights into other writing systems for both monolingual and bilingual children.
- Word-processing has enormous educational potential to raise the status of languages with non-Latin scripts and to develop skills in both composition and transcription. However, teachers need to be aware both of the limitations of various packages and of the very different needs of children and teachers.
- Teachers need to consider carefully a range of strategic, language and design issues in producing their own low budget resources.

6   A bridge to bilingualism

A bridge to bilingualism

The quality of resources in multilingual class-rooms is uneven. At one extreme, teachers' general level of awareness is very low. Their knowledge of the benefits of linguistic diversity – for individual children and for society as a whole – is limited and their focus is often exclusively on English. They may attempt to ban the use of other languages not only in the classroom but also in the playground; and they find the idea of encouraging children to read and write in their community languages anathema.

At the other extreme, many teachers' understanding of the issues is very high. They encourage the use of other languages throughout the school, secure in the knowledge that a firm foundation in the first language is essential for development in subsequent languages. Their approach is flexible and innovative. They have successfully identified the criteria for producing and evaluating effective learning materials and they put these into practice in their classrooms.

Between these two extremes lie the bulk of teachers in multilingual classrooms: professionals who understand the importance of acknowledging and valuing all the languages of their students, but who are often unsure as to which strategies will be most effective, which materials are available, or how best to address the gaps they have identified.

The Project has brought us into contact with many different teachers – monolingual and bilingual, mainstream and community. We have observed and talked to a wide range of children – monolingual and bilingual, British-born as well as more recent arrivals. We have reviewed a large number of materials, produced by teachers, parents and children as well as commercial publishers. What, then, are the conclusions to be drawn about using and producing multilingual resources for children?

Starting on a firm footing

One of our main findings is that the kind of initiatives which we have identified as good practice in this book can only be successful when the school has first addressed certain structural issues. For children to feel comfortable about using other languages, teachers need to create an atmosphere which not only acknowledges cultural and linguistic diversity but promotes it as a resource which benefits the school community as a whole.

A valuable first step is to examine the visual environment. There are many opportunities to feature the languages and cultures of the school in signs, posters, brochures, letters home, labels and home corners. If teachers hope to make parents welcome and comfortable, there also needs to be a policy of open access to classrooms. When parents are invited to exchange information and view their children's work in the morning or at the end of the day, the foundation is laid for a relationship of trust and mutual respect. Just as important is the need for a school policy on equal opportunities which addresses issues such as racist name-calling and the monitoring of performance, and which is clearly understood by teaching and ancillary staff and discussed openly with parents.

Speaking and listening

The most important resources for speaking and listening are, without doubt, bilingual members of the school community – teachers, ancillary staff, parents and, of course, the children themselves. The use of community or heritage languages is invaluable in many situations: in making new arrivals feel more comfortable; in explaining quickly and directly the meaning of a word or concept; in allowing children to have a clear understanding of the task in hand; in encouraging children to make inferences; in entertaining through stories, drama and role play. In all these situations, teachers offer children the opportunity to consolidate and extend their skills in their first language(s), thereby laying the foundation for sound development in the language of the school. They also send messages to monolingual children about the importance of bilingualism and about the similarities and differences between other languages and cultures.

In Project schools where other languages were clearly valued in both the visual environment and in the curriculum, the children we talked to – bilingual and monolingual – felt positive about the benefits of bilingualism.

In order to use bilingual skills effectively, it is important that teachers are well informed about the linguistic background of their students: which language(s) they speak at home; which languages they are studying in community classes. Teachers also have a responsibility to understand that naming practices vary enormously between one group and another and that mainstream conventions very often don't apply.

Bilingual teachers are clearly at an advantage when working with children from the same language background. However, monolingual teachers can also promote speaking and listening in other languages. Commercially produced tapes can be augmented with tapes recorded by parents and children. Bilingual parents can be encouraged to tell stories and work alongside children in the classroom. By allowing home language(s) in a range of different situations, affirming messages about the value of bilingualism are sent to all children.

Resources for reading

The main focus for *Building Bridges* has been books and reading. An important first step for teachers in meeting the reading requirements of bilingual children is to recognize that different cultural groups engage with text in different ways. In some societies, children are rewarded with books when they have learned to read rather than receiving them as an incentive to learn. In many societies, learning to read is approached through direct instruction which stresses repetition and rote learning.

The knowledge that the school's interpretation of reading is only one among many carries heavy responsibilities for the teacher. When children start school, they bring with them a picture of themselves as learners, based on all that has happened up to this point. Teachers need to find ways to acknowledge this outside-school experience. In order to do this, they need to create opportunities for discussing previous learning with children, their parents and others from the same background as the children.

A useful framework for this kind of discussion is the *Primary Language Record* (Barrs *et al.*, 1988) which records the whole range of the child's language experience from the perspective of teachers, parents and children themselves. Consulting children and parents not only provides useful information for the school; it also indicates that the teacher appreciates and understands the knowledge which children bring with them to formal education.

It is equally important that teachers make opportunities – when children start school, and at curriculum and parents' events – to explain to parents how they approach the teaching of reading. When your own experience of learning to read is very different, it is easy to misunderstand and feel confused about what is taking place in the classroom.

Teachers have a responsibility to be explicit about what they are doing and why.

Books in many languages

It is important to understand how different groups of people relate to the written word. Teachers who recognize that skills acquired in learning to read in one language are transferable to reading other languages will also be eager to provide opportunities for children to consolidate or extend literacy skills in their community languages.

Commercially produced books fall into two main categories: single language and dual language books. Many of the single language books are imported from the home country. They sometimes cause concern because they deal with experiences far removed from life in the new country and because the text is too difficult for children born abroad.

Books produced in countries like India, Pakistan and Bangladesh present an additional problem. Different standards of production result in a different feel which, according to some teachers, sends negative messages about the status of books in other languages. The children we consulted, however, suggest that such fears are unfounded. While the vocabulary they used demonstrated that they were aware of the differences, they insisted that their preferences were based on a number of factors, including the subject of the book and the quality of the illustration.

Dual language texts have given rise to even fiercer debate. Community teachers tend to dislike the use of English because they assume that children won't make the effort to read the community language. Mainstream teachers usually prefer dual language books because they can be used by both monolingual and bilingual readers.

Our observation and interviews in mainstream and community settings made it clear that teachers and children use dual language books in a variety of ways. For instance, it is possible to treat the book as a whole, or to take each page in turn, reading the first language, then the second. Children's comments were also illuminating. While some confirmed the suspicions of community language teachers that they read the English with little reference to the other language, others explained how they read the community language, referring only to the English when they encountered a word they didn't know.

Monolingual children also compared the two texts, often formulating interesting hypotheses about the differences between languages and scripts. Their speculation offers many valuable opportunities for discussion with teachers about the nature of linguistic diversity.

The design of bilingual children's books poses many challenges. It became apparent during the course of the Project that the suitability of a layout was closely related to how the reader intended to use the text. It was also clear that typographic features such as size and boldness of letter forms, the space between letters, words and lines, and whether typesetting, typing or handwriting is used to render the text, contribute to how the relative status of the two languages is perceived. When any of these variables is treated differently in the two languages, there is a risk that one of the texts will seem more important than the other. Since one of the main aims of introducing dual texts is to raise the status of other languages, it is self-defeating to use books where community languages are subordinated to English.

Another challenge concerns the treatment of directionality. When a dual language book draws on languages with different orientations on the page, what kinds of compromise are necessary? Books specifically designed as dual language texts sometimes overcome this problem in extremely inventive ways. Many, however, are adaptations of single language books where the addition of a second language sometimes results in design solutions which are far from satisfactory. The titles chosen for adaptation can also raise difficult questions. Some subjects make the journey from one language to another with greater ease than others.

The quality of translation is a related issue of considerable concern. All too often, the assumption has been that anyone who speaks another language has the necessary skills for translation. The reality is very different. A good translation depends on first-hand knowledge of the community language in question and familiarity with children's literature in English and the community language. It needs to be tested with both children and community language teachers to ensure that the level of difficulty of the translation matches the original text. Publishers also need to provide the same level of support to translators as they offer to writers in English, including access to copy-editing and proof-reading.

Writing as a resource

Monolingual teachers often lack the confidence to encourage writing in community languages, arguing that they don't have the necessary skills to evaluate or respond to children's work. These arguments are short-sighted. Children's writing need not be perfect: taking risks and making mistakes is an essential part in any learning process. Work intended for more public consumption can, of course, be checked by bilingual colleagues or parents.

There is growing recognition that literacy skills can be transferred from one language to another. While mainstream schools are not equipped to teach these various skills, they can provide opportunities for children to

develop the expertise acquired in the home country, in the family or at community schools. Book-making in other languages – by children and parents – was an activity which generated a great deal of excitement and enthusiasm in the Project schools we visited.

Learning to use the writing systems of other languages is useful for mono- and bilingual children. The non-Latin scripts of the Project languages demonstrate something of the variety of approaches to writing throughout the world. The logographic system of the Chinese, for example, where beginners have to learn hundreds of characters, provides an interesting contrast with a language like Urdu which is written in a script which has no vowels. The presence in the classroom of 'experts' in other writing systems can greatly extend monolinguals' understanding of the wide variety of approaches for making language visible.

In the course of the Project we found many examples of very effective handwritten stories illustrated with children's line drawings. We also saw exciting word-processed work by children which gives their other language the same status as English. However, teachers need to be aware of the various shortcomings of different programs. In some cases, characters sets are less than perfect; in other cases, low-resolution printers may make the script difficult to read and of low status.

We also saw the very real problems associated with producing low-budget resources in non-Latin scripts. Teachers attempting to meet the needs of a specific audience or to address gaps in teaching materials have to consider a range of strategic, language and design issues in producing child-friendly resources.

Worldview?

One of the important messages which we hope will emerge from this discussion is the need for international co-operation. Classrooms in which English co-exists with many other languages are the norm in large numbers of schools in North America, Europe and Australia. The observations we have offered have grown out of the experience of using multilingual resources for over a decade in British classrooms. We believe that many of the issues that have engaged British teachers are already – or will soon be – challenging educationalists in other countries.

Mainstream publishers are often reluctant to venture into multilingual resources because the markets are small and often difficult to locate. One possible way forward is to identify international rather than national markets. The Panjabi-speaking populations of Britain, the USA, Australia and Canada, for instance, are individually small but together represent a numerically much more significant group.

Another way forward is to identify specific projects where large sales will be assured. For instance, any books appearing on the SATs lists for national curriculum testing in British schools would be likely to sell well in any of the main community languages.

There are also possibilities for book sellers. Bookshops in areas of significant ethnic minority settlement need to be persuaded of the value of stocking books in the relevant community languages. Book distributors, too, need to be alerted to the possibilities of new markets. Books in other languages are, in the main, produced or distributed by a number of different small enterprises with small advertising budgets. It is very difficult for teachers to find out which resources are available and where. Book selections based on different languages drawing together titles from a range of publishers might prove a very attractive option for teachers responsible for book-buying.

We recognize that the current political agenda for education in the UK, with its

emphasis on national language and culture and its return to assimilationist policies (see Cameron & Bourne, 1988), may seriously curtail further development in this area. We look to colleagues in other parts of the world where budgets are perhaps more generous and the political climate less myopic and xenophobic for support in looking critically at both the production of resources and the ways in which they can be incorporated into classroom practice.

References

Abbott, C. (1994a) *Reading it: a teacher's guide to the use of computers in reading activities*. Reading: Reading and Language Information Centre, University of Reading

Abbott, C. (1994b) 'Supporting writing in community languages through the development and use of a multilingual word processor, and the involvement of community groups and parents in its use'. Paper given at the Sixth Conference on Computing and Writing, University of Wales, Aberystwyth

Alladina, S., & Edwards, V. (eds) (1991) *Multilingualism in the British Isles: Africa, the Middle East and Asia*. London: Longman

Baker, C. (1993) *Foundations of bilingual education and bilingualism*. Clevedon, Avon: Multilingual Matters

Barrs, M., Ellis, S., Hester, H. & Thomas, A. (1988) *The Primary Language Record*. London: Centre for Language in Primary Education

Barton, D. (1994) 'Sustaining local literacies'. Special issue of *Language and education*. vol. 8, nos. 1 & 2. Clevedon, Avon: Multilingual Matters

Bell, R. (1991) *Translation and translating: theory and practice*. London: Longman

Black, A. (1990) *Typefaces for desktop publishing: a user guide*. London: Architecture, Design and Technology Press

Brandt, H. (1945) *The psychology of seeing*. New York: Philosophical Library

Cameron, D. & Bourne, J. (1988) 'No common ground: Kingman, grammar and nation'. *Language and Education*, vol. 2, no. 3, pp. 147–60

Canadian Ethnocultural Council (1988) *The other Canadian languages: a report on the status of heritage languages across Canada*. Ottawa: Canadian Ethnocultural Council

Chatterji, M. (1991) 'Selection criteria for dual language books'. *Children's Book Foundation Spring Newsletter*, pp. 3–4

Cummins, J. (1994) 'The acquisition of English as a second language'. In K. Sprangen-Urbschat & R., Pritchard (eds) *Kids come in all languages: reading instruction for ESL students*. New Delaware: International Reading Association, pp. 36–62

Cummins, J. & Danesi, M. (1990) *Heritage languages: the development and denial of Canada's linguistic resources*. Toronto: Our Schools Our Selves and Garamond Press

Department of Education and Science (DES)(1988) *Report of the Committee of Inquiry into the teaching of the English language (The Kingman Report)*. London: HMSO

Devani, S. (1992) 'The Gujarati Folio project'. In National Council for Educational Technology, 'Look – my language is on the computer: information technology in the multilingual classroom'. Unpublished manuscript

Downie, R. A. (1963) 'Languages of the world that can be set on "Monotype" machines', *The Monotype Recorder*, vol. 42, no. 4

Edwards, V. & Redfern, A. (1988) *At home in school: parent participation in primary education*. London: Routledge

Edwards, V. & Redfern, A. (1992) *The world in a classroom: language in education in Britain and Canada.* Clevedon, Avon: Multilingual Matters

Fan, C. Y. (1981) *The Chinese Language School of San Francisco in relation to family integration and cultural identity.* Nanking, Taipei, Republic of China: Institute of American Cultural Academia Sinica

Feuerverger, G. (1994) 'A multilingual literacy intervention for minority language students'. *Language and Education,* vol. 8, no. 3, pp. 123–46

Fitzgerald, A. (1993) 'Tongues untied'. *Times Educational Supplement,* 28 May, p. 13

Ganly, T., Gilding, J. & Green, P. (1989) *Multilingual word processing.* Victoria, Australia: Statewide Multicultural Education Co-ordination Unit, Ministry of Education

Goldsmith, E. (1984) *Research into illustration: an approach and a review.* Cambridge: Cambridge University Press

Graves, D. (1983) *Writing: teachers and children at work.* London: HeinemannGregory, A., Redfern, A. & Lyons, H. (1991) *Writers' workshop: on becoming a writer.* Stoke-on-Trent: Trentham

Gregory, A., Redfern, A. & Lyons, H. (1991) *Writers' workshop: on becoming a writer.* Stoke-on-Trent: Trentham

Gregory, E. (1993) 'Reading between the lines'. *Tiimes Educational Supplement,* 15 October, p. 4

Hodgson, R. & Saronak, R. (1987) 'Graphic collisions: languages in conflict'. *Visible Language,* vol. 21, no. 1, pp. 18–41

Horvath, B. & Vaughan, P. (1991) *Community languages: a handbook.* Clevedon, Avon: Multilingual Matters

Kayembe, G. (1992) 'Words of honour'. In National Council for Educational Technology, 'Look – my language is on the computer: information technology in the multilingual classroom'. Unpublished manuscript

Keiner, J. (1991) 'The Hebrew speech community'. In S. Alladina & V. Edwards (eds) *Multilingualism in the British Isles: Africa, the Middle East and Asia.* London: Longman, pp. 239–52

Kenway, P. (1994) *Working with parents.* Reading: Reading and Language Information Centre, University of Reading

Kumar, R. (1988) 'Sharing texts: writing in two languages'. *The English Magazine,* vol. 21, pp. 36–8

Linguistic Minorities Project (LMP) (1985) *The other languages of England.* London: Routledge

Lubell, S. (1993) 'Bilingualism in the Hebrew text'. *Visible Language,* vol. 27, no. 1/2, pp. 163–204

Martin-Jones, M., Saxena, M., Chana, U., Barton, D. & Ivanic, R. (1992)*Bilingual resources in primary classroom interaction.* Working paper 53. Centre for Language in Social Life, University of Lancaster

McArthur, E. (1993) *Language characteristics and schooling in the United States: a changing picture.* Washington, DC: National Center for Education Statistics

National Council for Educational Technology (NCET) (1992) 'Look – my language is on the computer: information technology in the multilingual classroom'. Unpublished manuscript.

O'Grady, C. (1994) 'The guru and the beanstalk'. *Times Educational Supplement*, 11 March, p. 24.

Raby, R. (1991a) *Computers and Asian languages: a guide for community organisations on computing in the languages of the Indian sub-continent*. Oldham: Oldham Resource and Information Centre

Raby, R. (1991b) 'Asian language computer guide'. *Computanews*, no. 53, pp. 4–5

Ramirez, J. (1992) 'Summary of longitudinal study of structured English immersion, early-exit and late-exit transitional bilingual programs for language minority children'. *The Bilingual Research Journal*, no. 16, pp. 1–62

Routh, C. (1994) *See hear! A guide to audio-visual resources in the primary school*. Reading: Reading and Language Information Centre

Sampson, G. (1985) *Writing systems*. London: Hutchinson

Scarcella, R. (1990) *Teaching language minority students in the multicultural classroom*. Englewood Cliffs, NJ: Prentice-Hall

Smith, J. & Watkins, H. (1972) 'An investigation into some aspects of the illustration of primary school books'. Reading: Typography Unit, University of Reading

Street, B. (1984) *Literacy in theory and practice*. Cambridge: Cambridge University Press

Street, B. (1993) (ed.) *Cross-cultural approaches to literacy*. Cambridge: Cambridge University Press

Szanto, T. (1972) 'Language and readability'. *Icographic*, no. 3, pp. 18–19

Tsow, M. (1984) *Mother tongue maintenance: a survey of part-time Chinese language classes*. London: CRE

Urzúa, C. (1986) 'A children's story'. In P. Rigg & D. S. Enright (eds) *Children and ESL: integrating perspectives*. Washington, DC: TESOL, pp. 93–112

Walker, S. (1992) *How it looks: a teacher's guide to typography in children's books*. Reading: Reading and Language Information Centre and Department of Typography & Graphic Communication, University of Reading

Walker, S. (1993) *Desktop publishing for teachers*. Reading: Reading and Language Information Centre and Department of Typography & Graphic Communication, University of Reading

Wang, W. (1973) 'The Chinese language'. In *Human communication: language and its psychological bases. Readings from Scientific American* (no editor). San Francisco: WH Freeman & Co., pp. 52–62

Watts, L. & Nisbet, J. (1974) *Legibility in children's books: a review of research*. Slough: NFER Publishing Company Ltd

Wheatley, V. (1991) 'Using Panjabi Allwrite'. *Language and Learning*, vol. 5, pp. 2–4

Wheatley, V. (1991) 'Word processing in a nursery school'. In G. Keith (ed.) *Knowledge about language*. NCET, pp 33–42

Wong, L. (1991) 'The Hong Kong Chinese speech community'. In S. Alladina & V. Edwards (eds) *Multilingualism in the British Isles: Africa, the Middle East and Asia*. London: Longman, pp. 239–52

Wong, L. (1992) *The education of Chinese children in Britain: a comparative study with the USA*. Clevedon, Avon: Multilingual Matters

Index